The
Carny
Kid

The Carny Kid

Survival

of a

Young

Thief

My story by

Kenneth Kahn

10 9 8 7 6   5 4 3 2 1

ISBN 0-9761115-0-0

Library of Congress Control Number: 2004096680

Published by Pendant Press

Book layout and cover design by Ernie Weckbaugh of Casa Graphics, Inc., Burbank, California.

Manufactured in the United States of America by Thomson-Shore, Inc., Dexter, Michigan, USA.

ON THE COVER:
Upper right is the author as a toddler sitting on a carnival "Select Your Weight" scale. Below is a photo of his mother (left) in front of their booth at the carnival.

DEDICATION

This book is dedicated to every person
who has had to deal with "delinquent parents"

ACKNOWLEDGMENT

The person who most inspired me was my high school teacher, Mr. Raymond Lopez. Ray taught me many lessons through his enthusiastic instruction on so many subjects. It was his attitude, however, that made the deepest imprint. His influence on my education went well beyond school. He set an example of how to live life with zeal.

Raymond Lopez

TABLE OF CONTENTS

Introduction

Nothing in my 12 years on this planet had prepared me for the events leading to our family's move into the L.A. County Housing Projects in the spring of 1954.

We had been living on Alsace Avenue, a palm-lined street in a middle-class neighborhood known as West Adams, for about five years when the broken-down municipal moving van pulled up to collect our aging furniture that had been unceremoniously dumped onto the front lawn by the Sheriff's eviction squad a few hours earlier. Curious neighbors watched as two burly, unshaven movers clad in dirty overalls flung our few personal belongings into the back of the truck.

I only vaguely understood why we were being thrown out of our family home. It had something to do with 10 months of unpaid rent, apparently.

My Dad, Barry, was talking to the movers while Mom scrambled about trying to minimize the damage to our property. She carried my infant sister, Cookie, in one arm, while directing operations with the other. The two moving guys largely ignored her.

The baby was crying and squirming in Mom's arms. She had arrived only two weeks earlier after being released from County General Hospital where she had been born two months prematurely. One of our neighbor ladies, Mrs. Spitzer, who was visibly upset, offered to hold her. Mom readily accepted, then dashed back into our house to make a final inspection. On her return, she had our family pet, a duck named Squeeky Mae, under one arm and the cage in which she slept under the other. The duck, which I had brought home from the California State Fair in Sacramento two years earlier, quacked in alarm, as though she understood that all was not well.

My eight year-old brother, Ricki, stood by my side as we watched the last of the family's belongings being tossed onto the truck bed. "Why are they taking our stuff?" Ricki asked. "Did we sell it to them?" I put my arm around him and tried to reassure him, "Don't worry. We're just moving to a new house. It's still our stuff." I put on my bravest face because he looked up to me, but I was pretty shaken myself. I had no idea what was going on, but I knew it was nothing to celebrate.

When they were finished, the moving van driver growled, "We're done. Let's get outta here!"

Mom retrieved Cookie from Mrs. Spitzer, who was now crying openly, then handed the baby up to my brother who sat dazedly on our tattered sofa in the back of the truck. Mom climbed aboard and sat next to him. She held the baby while Ricki held the duck.

Dad and I headed towards his '39 Plymouth, which he referred to as the 'shitbox,' and started to get in when our former landlord, Mr. Wells, appeared on the front porch of the house and began to yell at us. "You low-life Jew bastards cheated me out of a year's rent. I hope you all rot in hell!"

Barry got out from behind the wheel, leaned over the hood of the car, and shouted back, "Everyone knows you left the country because you killed your wife. You belong in jail for murder!" Dad was referring to the local rumor that was going around the neighborhood, spread by nosey housewives.

Wells shot straight upright as though he had been struck in the ass by an electric cattle prod. His face was beet red with rage, in contrast to his shock of white hair. "I know what you do," he screamed. "You're nothing but a dirty 'DOPE FIEND!'"

The accusation rocked through my body with the certainty of its truth. A hundred unanswered questions I had while growing up were suddenly washed away. The strange visitors coming to the house in the middle of the night; the mysterious meetings in the bathroom; the acrid odors left in their wake now made perfect sense. I had seen movies in school about the "dope" underworld, and had been properly frightened. But this was the first time anyone had ever used the dreaded epithet "Dope Fiend" in my presence.

Wells' accusation was virtually confirmed when Dad flew into a maniacal rage and began to stomp menacingly across the front lawn towards Wells. He was seething and looking to inflict great bodily damage on the man. Instinctively, I realized that a nasty confrontation would worsen an already disastrous situation. Having played a lot of sandlot football in my day, I lunged for him and managed to tackle one leg as he strode across the yard. I failed to bring him down, instead holding on for dear life as he dragged me along with him towards Wells. "Don't do it, Dad," I pleaded. "It's not worth it. Let's just go."

The crowd of onlookers had grown in anticipation of

seeing a good fistfight. This kind of drama was not a common occurrence in our peaceful, middle-class neighborhood and would have made for some lively dinner conversation.

Dad's progress was slowed considerably by my dead weight on his lower leg. Finally, he looked down at me and realized that I was not about to release my grip. He relented and said, "O.K. You can let go. I don't need a probation violation anyway. Let's get the hell out of here."

We got back into the shitbox and tailed the moving van dutifully as it turned east on Adams Boulevard, heading towards downtown Los Angeles. I was still thinking about the "dope fiend" comment and what it meant for my life. I barely noticed the deteriorating quality of the buildings as we veered east through the city.

When I came out of my worrying for a moment, my mouth dropped. All around me were dilapidated structures with "For Rent" signs posted on their broken windows. Staggering winos inhabited the shadows between vacant stores. I wondered where we were going.

The "dope fiend" words rang in my head. I could not shake them loose. The images in the films shown at school just did not mesh with the life I had known with my parents.

The moving van spewed a steady stream of black exhaust that clouded the windshield of the Plymouth and forced us to roll up the windows. As we passed through downtown, I began to wonder just how bad neighborhoods could get. The signs on the streets were no longer in English. *Llantas usadas*, read one in front of a dirt-paved parking lot filled with rows of old tires piled six feet high.

When I finally cracked the car window to get some air, I noticed foreign aromas that caused me to wrinkle my nose. The odor of unwashed streets, together with the mixed smell of garbage and cooking grease, created a nasty fragrance. The people on the streets were shabbily dressed. Many gathered around vending carts selling some kind of unfamiliar food.

The events of the day were beginning to settle on me. I was having trouble sorting it all out. I wondered how long it would take to reach our destination, but now I hoped it wouldn't be too soon, given that I had not seen a single place that seemed remotely livable since we left our happy home in Ozzie Nelson land.

As the sun began to set, the moving van led us into a concrete and brick fortress known as 'public housing.' We descended the Lancaster Street hill into the Ramona Gardens Housing Projects. My nervousness turned to fear.

The crumbling walls of a dilapidated single-story building with cracking paint were covered with graffiti. *"Hazard Grande, con safos,"* one read. I didn't have a clue what it meant, but I guessed it didn't translate as, "Welcome little Jewish kid from the Westside."

At the entrance to the projects, at the northeast corner of Lancaster and Murchison, stood a cluster of tough-looking black guys, some pretending to spar with each other. Others were mimicking the words of a song blaring from a radio perched on a junked car.

On the opposite corner was an equally rough-looking gathering of young Mexicans. I studied them with concern as we drove by. They wore khaki pants and Pendleton shirts buttoned at the top. I could hear them speaking Spanish as they squatted in a semi-circle, smoking cigarettes.

None of these people resembled my playmates on Alsace Ave. It was hard to imagine playing ball in the street with them. It was hard to imagine talking to them or becoming friends. It was hard to imagine I was here at all. Although I had always been a pretty outgoing kid, I was in no great rush to meet them.

At last, the wobbly old moving van pulled into a parking lot behind 1342 Crusado Lane, one of a row of low-slung apartments that resembled a second-class military housing barracks, only not as nice. The driver of the van jumped out, approached the window of Dad's car and tersely said, "You're HOME."

Mom lowered herself from the back of the van and Ricki handed her the baby before jumping down himself. He reached back up to get the duck, which began squawking. Ricki held her tight to comfort her, but the quacking got louder. Dad and I exited his car and headed for the rear door of the apartment, where he used a key to unlock it.

As the door swung open, we were greeted by the sight of thousands of cockroaches scurrying about the kitchen floor. I had never seen a roach before and was not ready for the panorama of insects unfolding in front of me. I jumped back, accidentally giving my little brother a good whack on the head, nearly knocking him down.

16

Mom craned her neck in the doorway to get a glimpse of the interior, then recoiled in horror. "Get me out of here," she demanded. "Get me out of here right now!" She covered the baby's eyes and retreated to the Plymouth. "I'll never set foot in there," she stated in no uncertain terms.

Dad tried to calm her down. "OK. OK, no need to panic. We'll go somewhere else for the night. Tomorrow I'll come back with the boys and clean out the place. It'll be all right." I didn't know which "boys" he was referring to. Not me. I was staying with Mom.

I was sick to my stomach. The events of the day caught up with me and I went into overwhelm. I would run away. I'd become invisible. I'd kill myself. All these seemed like reasonable alternatives for me at the moment. I refused to acknowledge the nightmare my life had suddenly become. I fought back the tears welling up in my eyes. This had to be somebody else's life.

The rest of the family was equally repulsed. We piled into the old Plymouth and headed away as the movers began unloading our belongings. We didn't even stay to watch. It was almost 7:00 p.m. and the sun was barely visible in the sky, but I wasn't waiting for tomorrow. We drove in stunned silence. Then the baby began to cry. It was like she was expressing the feelings we were all hiding.

Dad found a fallen-down motel behind a taco stand near the corner of Marengo and Soto streets, not too far from the projects. He went inside and rented two rooms, one for him, Mom and the baby, one for Ricki, me and the duck. We had stayed in seedy motels before while traveling on the road for Dad's carnival business, but this place was an all-time low. It gave new meaning to the word "dump."

Dad led me to the room that my brother and I were supposed to share for the night. The rusty bed in the middle of the room sagged badly in the middle and the sheets were stained yellow. We tried our best to lie on it, fully clothed, but neither of us was willing to actually shut our eyes.

After about 15 minutes, Ricki and I left our room and took the duck to the room where the others were staying. I was nearly in tears when Dad opened the door. "We want to stay with you guys. That other room is terrible."

That night, all five of us slept in the same bed, clutching each other for reassurance. No one got much sleep.

The Summer of '41

Our family's fortunes had not always been so down-trodden. Back in the summer of 1941, there was just the three of us, Mom, Dad and their new infant son, me. We were living in Ocean Park, a seaside resort located between Santa Monica and Venice Beach. A bustling wooden jetty called Lick Pier extended out to sea from the boardwalk a quarter of a mile long, all the way to a giant rollercoaster that serpentined out over the Pacific Ocean.

Ocean Park offered the hottest entertainment in Los Angeles, and Lick Pier was the heart of the action. With two ballrooms, each able to accommodate 2,000 swinging young people, every night was a party. Name bands played both dance halls and attracted standing-room only crowds.

Between the Casino Ballroom at the foot of the pier and the Aragon Ballroom at the very end were rides and carnival games of all sorts. World War II was on the American horizon, and so the general attitude was somewhere to the left of 'WHOOPEE.' Crowds of revelers poured onto the pier each night to cavort and dance away. The thrill rides had long lines, the dance halls were overflowing, and the games of chance were raking in loot as quickly as it could be separated from the oblivious suckers.

Among the underground colony of hipsters making a killing in and around Lick Pier, none was more aggressive than my Dad, Barry Kahn. It almost seemed that our family name was aptly fitting. A sharp opportunist with an eye for an easy buck, he never met a scam he didn't like. Barry often bragged that he "had never worked an honest day in his life."

Barry made his entry onto the scene when he acquired one of the gaming joints on the pier in a rigged card game. Since hustling dice and cards were his stock-in-trade, he had little trouble relieving one of the local sharpies of his money and the ownership of a game of chance on the 'midway.' Suddenly the 30-year old fugitive from the underworld of San Francisco found his pot of gold. What began as a single joint soon became three, producing a steady stream of cash that made picking pockets unnecessary. He was living the good beach life, had hip friends, a beautiful wife (as well as a few lady friends on the side) and a new baby boy as well. Life was good.

PART I

Barry

Barry was born Myron Barry Cohen in July, 1911, the twelfth child out of 13 to be born to Romanian-Jewish immigrants. His dad was a hard-working carpenter whose *good* luck was to have a brilliant first-born son, my Uncle Jack, but whose *bad* luck was to then have TEN GIRLS in a row. Getting the daughters married became the household obsession. Everything depended on good marriages for the daughters. The last two kids, my dad and his younger brother, George, were almost an afterthought.

Although Grandpa Cohen was wiped out in the San Francisco earthquake, he worked very hard and rebuilt a respectable life for his family. There may have been a presumption that Barry would emulate his older brother's success in the business world, and therefore require little supervision. But that notion was disabused as young Barry created a scene everywhere he went. He loved to start fights. He was thrown out of every school he ever attended. He cut classes, stole clothes to wear, smoked cigarettes, and hung out with local wiseguys who taught him to pick pockets and cheat at cards and dice.

He was eventually sent to a boy's reformatory, but was thrown out there, too. By the end of the ninth grade, his school life was a thing of the past. His more useful education on the streets proceeded unhindered as he became an accomplished small-time thief of some repute.

He tried his hand at professional boxing. The problem was, while he could have done well as a young lightweight, he preferred street fighting where he got extra enjoyment out of beating guys up, especially big guys. He would go out of his way to lure some brute into a fight and then box his ears.

Barry's role models were the Hollywood tough guys of the day— George Raft, Bogie, Cagney—all sharp guys in double-breasted suits with silk ties, money in their pockets, and no visible means of support. These were the guys who managed to outsmart the system—fast women, fast cars, and fast money.

Barry learned a wide assortment of scams, and he was quite inventive in creating his own as well. For instance, one Christmas he brazenly ripped off one of San Francisco's finest department stores. It was a busy Saturday afternoon and the store was filled with holiday shoppers. Long lines of children anxiously waited to see Santa Claus. Women swarmed all the cosmetic counters. The sporting-goods department had half its inventory spread across the floor. Store employees, including many temporary holiday hires, were at a loss as to how to handle the crowd.

Peggy Slater, one of the new employees in the candy section, was approached by a good-looking, slender young man. He was well-dressed in dark slacks and a white shirt, with the cuffs rolled up. He wore an official badge reading "SECURITY" and carried a canvas bank bag and a receipt book.

"Collections," he announced. "Clean out the cash drawer, please. Put all large bills in this bag." He held out the canvas sack on which "Bank of America" was emblazoned. Peggy blinked, "Is this part of store operations? They never mentioned collections during my briefing."

"It's part of our new security regulations, Miss," he responded. "Cuts down on the temptation to steal." He tightened his tie and pulled out a receipt book. "How much is in the register?" he inquired as he began to write in the book. Peggy counted out $340.00 and placed in the bag. He completed a cash receipt in that amount and handed it to her. "Keep it in the bottom of your cash drawer," he cautioned. Then, flashing his most winning smile, he offered, "By the way, are you free after work? There's an employee party later. It's only for permanent workers, but I can get you in if you want." She smiled back and said, "Sure. When does it start?" He said, "I'll meet you at 6:00 under the clock at the main entrance."

Peggy watched as the flirtatious security officer made his way over to the men's wear department and began to speak to a new employee at the cash register there. Then she had to wait on a new customer.

The canvas bag was nearly full by the time the young man headed toward the main cashier's office. But he never got there. Instead, he ducked out of the store and into the street, the bag stuffed securely in his pants. He began to whistle "Jingle Bells" as he strolled away.

"For a Jewish guy, it's amazing how much I love the Christian holidays," he thought.

22

Faye

In the early 1900s, Philip Brodinsky and his wife Tillie settled into the Strawberry Mansion district of Phliadelphia. As one of Philly's oldest neighborhoods, the Mansion district was destroyed by the British in 1777. By 1781, the property was taken over by none other than Benedict Arnold. The premises then devolved to a couple of judges who improved the property—Judge Lewis in 1791, and Judge Hemphill who added two Gothic wings in 1828. By the start of the Civil War in 1860, the Mansion was purchased by the City of Philadelphia. The area soon became a leading cultural center of the city.

Between 1881 and 1930, a Jewish quarter developed and flourished. When Czar Alexander II of Russia was assassinated on March 1, 1881, his successor, Alexander III, sought revenge against the Jews, thereby triggering a mass exodus to the west. Among those seeking refuge from the Czar's purge was young Philip, now known as Brody. He made his way tortuously over the face of Europe to England. On the journey he met and married Tillie Rose, a Polish refugee. Together they sought safety in the U.S.

After a few unsuccessful attempts at entering the business world, Philip bought a horse and cart and began to deliver vegetables throughout the city. His new venture was successful enough to permit the support of his wife and four children, and entry into the promising world of the newly emerging Jewish community in Strawberry Mansion.

By 1934, Grandpa Phil had established himself in the neighborhood. A good-looking brute of a guy, he had a reputation as a ladies' man, or as the local Jews noted, a "ladygeyer" in Yiddish. He had the uninhibited habit of bringing his female friends to the family home, where he would escort them to his bedroom and demand that his wife prepare a meal for them. Poor Tillie was so brutalized by him that she complied without a word. The kids fumed, but there was little they could do.

He dominated his children with force and fear. His first born, Sarah, was the primary recipient of his brutality. He would enter the house in a bad mood and routinely proceed to smack her around. His second born was Hymie, who received the same treatment which led to his becoming a carbon copy of his father. Phil's third child, Nathan, caught a little less of his father's rage but plenty enough to develop a venal hatred of him. Only Fanny, the baby, was spared. She spent most of the time in the kitchen with her mother. It was a favorable defensive position to avoid the blows freely distributed to her siblings. The net result was a household gripped by fear and loathing of the old man.

Fanny, my mom, was spared the worst of the physical abuse, but developed the most vitriolic hatred of her father. She reviled him throughout his life and for decades after his death. She vowed to never associate with any man who was essentially a "disgusting pig."

Like her older brothers and sister, Fanny discarded her old-world name and became "Faye." Hymie became Herman, and eventually "Steve." Sarah became "Sally" and Nathan became "Nate." The kids plotted against their father, hoping to force his exit from the family home. By the time Faye was 13, the children had convinced Tillie to throw Philip out. The boys were big enough to make a stand physically, and all the kids were prepared to help out financially. Their plot worked and Phil finally left.

Faye graduated from Fitzsimon Junior High School in June, 1930, and went to work in a clothing factory. Her formal education was over. That year she met Freddy, who was to become her boyfriend. For the next six years they were virtually inseparable. He was the best thing that ever happened to her, and everyone who knew them naturally assumed they would marry.

And so it came to pass that their wedding date was set for June, 1938. Except for one tiny glitch, the marriage would have come off as planned. The night before the ceremony, Faye went to her mom and announced that she could not go through with it. She had no explanation for her change of mind. "I can't tell you exactly why, " she confessed. "I just know that I can't marry Freddy." And that was the end of the discussion.

That night, Faye and Tillie scoured the whole of Strawberry Mansion for every dollar, dime and penny they could scrape together. Friends and relatives contributed enough money to send their 21-year-old Faye, who had developed into a fine looking, busty young woman, across the country on a Greyhound Bus to seek a new life.

Her mom gave her the name and address of a distant relative living in Los Angeles who might be willing to take her in. And so it was that the fresh young girl, on her first trip out of Philadelphia, and her first trip anywhere outside of her mother's kitchen, stood nervously at the front door of the address that had been given to her.

Freida and Schlomo Glotz gave Faye an icy welcome. "You can sleep on the couch 'til you get a job. And when you do, you'll bring the pay envelope home unopened," Freida stated flatly. "Understood?" Schlomo added. Faye agreed and so began her new life on the West Coast.

Her spartan regimen proved to be pretty dismal. She found work as a counter girl at Comets, the original Orange Julius stand in downtown L.A. She put in her shift six days a week, and turned in the paycheck unopened. It seemed like one long unending treadmill. She was virtually an indentured servant to her "jailer" second cousins, once removed.

Her opportunity to break free came as a result of tips. She had squirreled away a few coins here, a few coins there, and they soon added up. She was able to save enough to rent a room and truly set out on her own.

Several months later she wrote her older sister. "Dear Sally, you really must come to California. My life was pretty stinky for awhile, but it's just fine now. I have my own place and you could stay with me, or we could get a bigger place. Either way, it's better than Strawberry Mansion. I beg you to come out. Love, Faye."

Big sister came out and the two girls moved into larger quarters. It was the beginning of a new chapter in their young lives. Freedom. Freedom as never before. Freedom to come and go as they pleased. Freedom from parental oversight, and freedom to choose a whole new set of values, to be a little crazy.

The Meeting

The Italian Village was a hopping underground bar in central L.A. Steps led from the street level down into the smoke-filled, noisy cavern. One Friday night, Faye and Sally were in one corner of the club, allowing themselves to be hustled by a couple of "older" guys, like in their forties. The men were free spenders and treating the girls to whatever they wanted. In Philadelphia, the sisters had never learned the art of getting men to buy them things, but they were learning fast now. Both of them were looking their best that evening and having no trouble attracting admiring glances from men at nearby tables.

Strolling into the club at that moment was one cutting-edge hipster just in from Frisco. Wearing a double-breasted suit topped with a Stingy-brim fedora, he resembled a small version of Cesar Romero. Slicked back hair — jet black – with a pencil thin moustache. A killer of a man, it was Barry Kahn, the devil in disguise.

He cruised through the club looking for an easy lay. Loose girls were Barry's type. In fact, he had never known any other type. When he spotted the girl in the scoop-necked white blouse with a gardenia in her upswept hair, he came to a grinding halt. She did not have the dime-store quality he was used to. She had a special glow, the kind of radiance that only comes from innocence. Definitely not his type, yet there was a powerful attraction he could not explain. He determined to make a move.

Barry stalked back and forth across the bar waiting for an opening. He got his chance when Faye went to the powder room. He accosted her in a small hallway near the coatroom. "Hi, haven't I met you somewhere before?" he inquired, leaning into her as he spoke. She backed away and replied, "Isn't that a pretty weak line?" He stood fully upright and bowed deeply, "Of course it is. I have some that are much better. May I try them out on you?"

"Not right now," she demurred. "We already have a full table as you can see." She gestured towards her sister and the two guys. As she retreated into the ladies' room, he called after her, "Full tables have never been a problem for me."

When she exited the powder room, Barry was standing right where she had left him, waiting for her. He took her by the arm and escorted her back to the table. "Hi, I'm Barry," he announced to the group. He put an arm around Mom. "We're old friends. Mind if I join you?" Without waiting for an answer, he snagged a chair from another table and inserted himself between the two girls.

Things went from bad to worse for the two guys buying the drinks as Barry proceeded to dominate the conversation. Unfortunately for the guys, his stories were funny and the girls laughed aloud in gay approval.

Abruptly, one of the guys stood up and declared, "We'd better get going if we're going to catch the late show at Monty's." He reached for Sally's chair. "We promised a show to the girls," he explained to Barry. His partner said, "I'll go hail a taxi." They all got up and headed towards the stairs leading up to the street.

Unrelenting, Barry trailed up the stairway after them, trying to get Faye's phone number as they exited the club. Before she could reply, the taxi appeared. As the girls entered the back seat of the cab, Barry insinuated himself between them, leaving the two guys to cram in front next to the driver. The girls looked perplexed, the guys in front depressed, leaving Barry with a big smile as the party charged on.

Once at Monty's, Barry slipped the doorman $10 to expand the reservation from four people to five. Now they were all one big, happy family.

Needless to say, Barry did get Faye's phone number and they had their first date the following night.

First Date

Barry rolled up in a shiny new car to the apartment house where Faye and Sally shared a room. Wearing a snappy suit and matching hat, he was dashing to the point that he found it unnecessary to mention that the car was recently removed from a parking lot around the corner without the permission of the owner.

He drove to a swank restaurant in Hollywood where he made a point of laying a few bucks on the maitre'd, the hat check attendant, and the girl selling cigarettes. Faye noted all of this with awe. This guy was something else.

Barry was the perfect escort that evening. After dinner, he drove to Central Avenue, the center of the hot, black jazz scene that was the rave in that era. They entered Club Alabam where he seemed to be well known. Faye had never been to an all-black club. She began to sense that there must be a whole world out there that she knew absolutely nothing about. They had drinks and listened to hot jazz.

On the way home, the conversation took a sudden turn when Barry blurted, "I want to marry you." Faye blinked, "Did I hear you right?" "Absolutely," he responded. "We're made for each other. There's no point in fighting it. We could wait and wait, and do all the usual 'courting' stuff, but it's not necessary. We're going to wind up getting married anyway."

Faye sat bolt upright. "I can't believe what you're saying. I hope this is a joke."

"I'm dead serious," Barry asserted. "What's the point of dragging out something that you KNOW is going to happen eventually." She edged towards the car door. "STOP RIGHT NOW," she demanded. "I want out. You're a nut case."

Sensing that things were not going well, Barry backed off. "OK, OK, don't get so upset. I just thought we could get on with our lives together without going through all the rigamarole." Faye turned beet red and demanded, "I said stop the car. I want out and I never want to see you again."

Barry began slowing the car, but did not stop. He knew he had overplayed his hand and needed time to clean it up.

"I'm sorry," he said. "I promise I won't bring up the subject again." She retorted, "I don't care what you do. Whatever it is, it's not going to have anything to do with me. STOP THIS CAR NOW!"

He slowed more. "Just give me another chance," he pleaded. "I made a mistake. I give you my word you'll never again hear the subject of marriage from my lips." Unfortunately, Faye had no idea of what Barry's "word" was worth and began to relent. "Well, if you give me your solemn promise..." Barry sensed her weakening. "My word of honor. Just forget this entire conversation. It'll never come up again. I promise. We'll just get on with our lives."

A year later, to the day, they were married in Tijuana, Mexico.

A Different World

During their "courting" year, Barry showed young Fanny a world she could not have imagined. He seemed to have an unending coterie of friends. Every day, she met someone new. They were straight out of Damon Runyan's cast of underworld characters. None of them had a regular job. Nobody had a permanent address, preferring to move from one hotel room to another. Everyone slept at least until noon. There never appeared to be a shortage of spending cash. They were up all night partying or running off to some mysterious rendezvous that was not discussed or explained.

This routine changed only minimally. Almost without exception, there was a late-night meeting at one of the Central Avenue jazz spots. Faye was soon introduced to the secret world of "reefer," also known as "boo" or "grass." Someone would produce a brown hand-rolled cigarette and they would slip out a side door to fire it up. The stuff had a strange smell, and she initially refused to partake. But eventually her curiosity got the better of her and she gave it a try. To her surprise she liked it. It was relaxing and opened a part of her mind that had always been hidden for her. It also felt good … and sexy. There appeared to be some sort of symbiotic relationship between the reefer and the music. She began to love jazz.

And there was laughter. Everyone cracked up at Barry's improvisational monologues. He was aided by his main partner in crime, Reed Kimball, who had a lightning wit of his own. They would spend hours trying to outdo each other or simply playing off each other's bits. Together they had the party in stitches. Sometimes people actually fell off their chairs, holding their sides, begging them to stop.

Faye opted to avoid examining any of this scene too closely. The questions she had about where the money was coming from were none of her business. She had her suspicions, but it caused her little concern. She was too enthralled with the lifestyle to ask. Barry had persuaded her to give up her square job, and quitting it was just fine with her. She allowed herself to be swept up in his renegade approach to life and she was digging it. Why ask unnecessary questions?

The reality of the situation came into focus one evening when the two of them were strolling down the street with her on the inside and him nearest the street. A well-dressed, obviously inebriated gentleman was staggering down the street in the opposite direction. As they passed each other, Barry reached across her and lifted the drunk's wallet. He did it so smoothly, he hardly lost a step and Faye barely noticed. The hapless victim also hadn't a clue. Barry quickly removed a fat wad of cash and dumped the wallet into a trashcan. "So, where shall we go for dinner?" he inquired, nonchalantly.

Faye was speechless, but she allowed herself to be steered into a passing taxi. They were soon dining on thick steaks and fine wine. The fact that Barry was such an accomplished pickpocket only enhanced his aura of invincibility. After all, he only stole from those who could well afford it. It was like an elaborate game. No one really got hurt and the lifestyle it afforded them was super.

Ocean Park

During the war years in the 1940s, Ocean Park in Santa Monica was THE place to be. In those days, you could take the streetcar from the center of downtown L.A. to the beach in one straight shot. You jumped on the P car that ran down Pico Boulevard and in a single no-muss, no-fuss ride, you could shoot straight to the Pacific and the candy-apple attractions of Ocean Park and the midway on the pier.

The beach and the ocean were tremendous draws in and of themselves. The classic beauty of sunny, Southern Californian white sand beaches in conjunction with the raucous nightlife was a dynamite combination.

The amusement pier was devoted exclusively to fun 'n games — games for kids, adults, and even games for old people.

There was always something to do. The boardwalk was filled with its own diversions including bars and restaurants, hotels with swimming pools, and lots of single young people looking for a good time.

As the war progressed, the scene was increasingly dominated by servicemen of all types hoping to have what might turn out to be their last good time ever. Soldiers and sailors had money to burn. No point worrying about saving when you're scheduled to ship out to some God-forsaken broiling island in the south Pacific to engage in a life-or-death battle.

Along with the military came the U.S.O., where G.I.s could meet local girls to talk to, dance with, take for a ride on the monster roller-coaster and, if lucky, share a boat ride through the Tunnel-of-Love.

The two local dancehalls located on Lick Pier attracted the biggest of the big bands, and were the premier attractions. Duke Ellington, The Dorsey Bros., Artie Shaw, Cab Calloway, made an already happening scene into a Great Happening.

The pier truly was just one ongoing party. There was a surplus of everything good and fun at a time when fun was desperately needed. Even at 3:00 or 4:00 a.m., there were still people out on the waterfront boardwalk talking politics or sports, hanging out waiting for sunrise, or just too drunk to get home. It was an insomniac's dream. The scene had everything—including predators.

In between the ballrooms and the cotton candy stands were scattered various games of chance. "Step right up, partner, let's see if you can win the little lady one of these adorable cupie dolls. Don't you worry none miss, I'm sure that your big, strong man can knock over some itty-bitty milk cans. That'll be a quarter, sir."

Many quarters came and went, yet the cupie doll still sat in the same spot. "Hey, wait a minute, how come no one ever wins?" Because this was carny-land. A place where easy marks abounded. Suckers were everywhere. Just throw up some phony scam game that's totally rigged for the house to win, and watch the marks throw their money away.

Whether the game involved balls or darts or pitching coins, they were all designed to separate cash from unsuspecting prey. It wasn't so much a lot of money taken from one person, but rather small amounts pilfered from lots of people. When you spread it out, it wasn't so bad.

And the carnies loved it. It was like free money! It wasn't even illegal, except maybe a little. People had fun trying to win, and it was borderline justifiable as a sort of entertainment surcharge. It provided a tax-free income to dozens of petty thieves. And a pretty darned good income at that. The lizards were ridin' high.

Barry owned one game, but soon graduated to own two and then three. He hired agents to put on an apron and work the counters. With three sets of employees to look after, he had to keep hustling just to keep track of how much money they were stealing from him.

In addition, Dad had wormed his way into the U.S.O., where soldiers and sailors would congregate for a break in the action. He convinced the authorities to let him install pinball machines as recreation for the servicemen.

Late at night, after the pier closed down, Barry and Faye would empty the machines, and then arrive home with bulging sacks of nickels and dimes. They invited their friends over to help them roll up the coins into paper wrappers. Every night, the sound of coins and partying filled the air.

After a couple of stays at different beachside hotels, the young couple rented a small one-bedroom back-house at $49^{1/2}$ Ozone Ave. It had a fair-sized combo living room / kitchen area that could hold eight to ten late-night revelers. Located only a half-block from the boardwalk and two blocks from the pier, everyone could walk to the house. The party lasted until either dawn or the last person passed out.

My Arrival

7

Faye Kahn tossed and turned miserably on her hospital bed in the Cedar's of Lebanon Hospital in the morning hours of June 17, 1941. Her pregnancy had been difficult and now the delivery was worse. The unborn child was not co-operating. The head was in the wrong position and the doctor advised that he might have to open her up and perform a C-section.

The pain was awful as she writhed upon the sweaty sheets. The nurses seemed singularly unconcerned about her stressed condition, as they scurried from one patient's room to another. "Where is Barry?" she wondered as she thrashed about trying in vain to find a comfortable position. "The nurse told me he called and said he was on his way." But that was hours ago. There was no way for her to know that he was involved in the final stages of a hot dice game. He was down, and not about to leave 'til he got even. He didn't.

Eventually they had to open Mom up, and still it was no easy task to extricate the baby. I had gotten too comfortable in my warm home. The doctor relied on a pair of forceps to pull me out from my hiding place. He tugged and yanked until I popped out, incidentally leaving a scar over my right eye, which would be my faithful companion for life. It may have been a sign of events to come. If I had any idea of what I was in for I would have fought harder to stay.

At last, Dad arrived and pretended to be overjoyed. My birth was greeted with mixed feelings. I came at a point in their lives when they simply had no time or interest in being parents.

They responded to the situation by letting the new addition interfere as little as possible with their routines. Within a couple of months they returned to their former lifestyle.

Faye was rapidly becoming "Queen of the Ballroom," as she physically matured into a beautiful woman and Barry returned to his petty larceny, which was paying off quite well. They each had their own interests, and being in any way good, domestic parents was not on the agenda. Between sleeping until 2:00 p.m. and having a series of babysitters thereafter, they found it was nearly possible to ignore the baby altogether.

The earliest memories I have go back to the birth of my brother, Ricki. Born three-and-a-half years after me, he immediately became the second unnecessary addition to the family. By the time he was six months old, he was given to me to be his primary caretaker. Faye showed me how to give him his bottle, change his diaper, and bathe him. I was a quick learner and soon had complete responsibility for his well-being. It got so that I hated my brother. I hated my mother and father as well by this time, but Ricki was the one who was always there. I felt like strangling him.

I virtually never saw either of my parents. They gave me strict instructions NEVER to wake them before two in the afternoon, NEVER let them hear my brother cry, and DON'T MAKE ANY NOISE! These were the only rules I was given. Ever. I was on my own and had to figure out what to do with my life.

I got my big break one year later when I started kindergarten. I was ready for school; I knew the alphabet and could read some of the words in the newspaper. I'm not sure how I learned, but I had a fascination with words and studied the newspaper every morning at the kitchen table while my parents slept.

In the fall of 1946, Mom took me by the hand to the corner of Ozone Avenue and the "Speedway" which was the main street running alongside the beach. We got on the bus, headed south a few stops, and got off at Sunset Ave. She showed me Sunset School and took me inside to register me.

On the way home, she turned to me and said, "That's your new school. Tomorrow I'm going to give you money for the bus and you can go by yourself. OK?" I nodded assent.

That was the last time anyone ever took me to school. I didn't mind. It was easy and I could tell that she couldn't be bothered. Most importantly, I got to get away from my brother. Plus, I loved school from the very first day.

I was shocked to find a place where the adults actually talked to you. There were toys and games and things to learn.

There were other kids to play with. They gave you cookies and you had to take a nap. I never wanted to leave. It was by far the best part of my life.

After school, I returned home and roamed the beachfront. I played alone in the cold waters of the Pacific, and had an undercurrent nearly wash me away several times. I quickly learned to respect the sea.

I wandered alone up and down the pier when I was done amusing myself on the beach. Everyone knew who I was and offered me candy and soft drinks. I was a regular at Harry's Delicatessen. With no one to supervise me, I began hanging out at the newspaper stand at the foot of the pier. It was run by an old guy who had a hip ailment that caused him to walk with a severe limp. The locals, lacking sensitivity, nick-named him Hippy. I hung out with him a lot. We were both outcasts and found solace in each other's company.

One day, out of boredom, I asked Hippy if I could sell papers for him. He agreed, and gave me an apron to keep change in and a handful of newspapers. I had my first job at age five.

The business world opened new vistas for me. First, and foremost, it gave me a purpose in life. I had responsibility. I had papers to sell. I had to deal with money. I was some-body. I could go into restaurants and bars and talk to the patrons. The customers, especially those in the bars, seemed to like me. The older men would sit me on a barstool and order me a ginger ale. The women would get protective and hug me to their breasts, which I didn't mind at all.

And I was selling newspapers like mad. Three or four times an afternoon, I would return to the stand to turn in my money and get more papers. Hippy was amazed and pleased. I found out later that he was cheating me out of my commis-sion. My dad was the one who brought it to my attention. But I really didn't care because I wasn't in it for the money. It did show me that someone could cheat a little kid who had limited math skills and an unquestioning trust in adults. Nevertheless, I would have gladly worked for free. I loved the attention.

Sometimes I would wake up early, around five or six in the morning, and wander out to the deserted pier. I was particularly attracted to the red fire alarm box on the wooden post near the Fun House. One day, I pulled the handle to see what would happen. The alarm went off with an incredibly loud, clanging, bell. I ran like the wind to get away. I sensed that I had done something wrong and was terrified of getting caught.

But I ended up being not so terrified that I stopped doing it. It came to be an obsession with me. Every once in awhile, when the temptation became too great, I returned to the early morning scene of the crime to repeat my dastardly act of rebellion.

I never got caught, at least not by the police. One morning as I was about to pull the alarm, I was surprised by an old vagrant. He said he knew that I was the one who had set the false alarms in the past. I panicked and ran into the House of Mirrors. He followed me. I knew the floor plan fairly well because I had sneaked in there in the past. I had no idea what he intended to do with me. Sheer terror shot through my body as he chased me through the mirrored hallways. I don't have a clear recollection of exactly what happened next, but I do recall it was the last time I made an early morning sojourn to the pier. The incident in the House of Mirrors haunted me for years. I believe I was sexually assaulted, but even after years of therapy as an adult, I could not remember what happened that day.

Other than this incident and the two times the undercurrent nearly pulled me under, I had a good time wandering freely on the boardwalk.

The Bubble Bursts

The end of WWII precipitated the end of Ocean Park as the mega-entertainment complex by the sea. America was back on wheels. Civilian vehicles were not made during the war years, and so there arose a huge demand for automobiles immediately after the war. Giant amusement parks had had their day. The G.I.'s who had been the lifeblood of the action were gone. Only the hangers on and the old Jews stayed behind.

This was all very bad news for the hipsters like Dad. No suckers, no money. End of story. Time to move on. But to where? Where could one find an abundance of easy marks? No longer in Ocean Park.

During this transition, Barry found himself at the wrong end of a major car wreck. He and his buddy were stopped at a red light on Culver Blvd in front of Stearns Barbeque, when a stolen car being pursued by the police swerved onto the wrong side of the road. The car smashed head on into Dad's car, and the cop car ran into a phone pole that then collapsed on them. When the final tally was in, everyone but Barry died in the crash.

Dad was given a very slight chance of survival. He had cracked every rib in his body. His nose was flattened against his face, which had smashed through the windshield. He had contusions, cuts, and bleeding from half a dozen spots. He was given 24 hours to live. When he made that deadline, they extended their estimate to 48 hours. After numerous surgeries though, they cautiously upgraded his condition. There was a massive reconstruction of the nose to be done.

Barry beat the odds. His toughness allowed him to survive. But there was a tragic permanent injury that would never go away. During the course of his recovery, the doctors had provided him with as much morphine as he wanted. It was an extremely long and painful period, made bearable only by the use of heavy narcotics.

When Barry was finally released from the hospital, he was completely addicted. It was an addiction that was to run his life for the next thirty years.

Meanwhile, the stay in the hospital left our family nearly destitute. He had no insurance, and the guy who hit him had been driving a stolen car. All the money from the heyday of the pier was gone. It was time to find a new scam.

While Barry was recovering from the accident, he ran into an old friend of his from the Pier, "Balloonhead" Bill. Bill was a tall, lanky guy with a huge hook nose who specialized in running balloon games in Ocean Park. Bill told Barry about his recent experience with a traveling carnival. "Man, it's the same scam as on the Pier, except you go from town to town with the show," he explained as Barry listened intently. "You go from one county fair to another. Nothing but farmers with fat wads of cash just waiting to be taken. I made a lot of money last season."

Bill continued, "They have some games on the show that I've never seen before, games that win a lot of money. I saw one agent beat a mark for $4,000."

Barry was incredulous. "How's that possible on a carnival lot? I never heard of such a scam."

"Oh yes, it's possible. They got a joint called a 'flat store' that beats any carnival game I've ever seen. It's the best designed theft device ever. It's so slick the carnival hires a guy to bribe the local sheriffs wherever they go. They call him the 'Patch Man.' Probably the most important man on the lot. Thanks to his payoffs, he allows the show to run these high-powered games."

Barry inquired, "What happens if the mark wises up to the scam or gets out of hand?"

"That's where our friend the sheriff steps in. He simply tells the mark, 'Hey, it's a game of chance, pal. You knew that 'Billie Joe' when you went into it. It's gambling. Sometimes you win, sometimes you lose. You lost. Go home! Have a beer and give your old lady a jump. You'll feel a whole lot better.'"

"I'm ready to give it a shot," Barry exclaimed. "Where's the next spot. I'm coming with you." So began a lifelong career on the road for Barry and his family.

The Bloody Exit

One night I was sleeping in my bed across from my little brother. I was awakened by loud voices shouting from the living room. I heard a female scream. Then I recognized the voices. One of them was Dad and the woman was Mom. The other was this kid named Ronnie, a youngster who was Dad's protégé. He was learning the ins and outs of the underworld from the master. Now he was caught in the middle of a life-or-death drama.

Barry had come home from the road unexpectedly, in the middle of the night. He had caught the two of them in *flagrante delicto* on the bed. He had an unobstructed view from the front window. He kicked open the door and burst into the room screaming, "You rotten whore. I'll kill you both!"

The two lovers jumped off the bed and protested their innocence, begging for mercy. Barry dashed to the kitchen where he had stashed his gun. He found the weapon, pulled it out and aimed it at the kid. I could hear Ronnie begging, "Barry, Barry, don't kill me! Don't shoot. Don't shoot."

Mom screamed, "Put down the gun. We weren't doing anything."

Barry was crazed, "I've got eyes. I know what I saw. I'll kill both of you. I'll kill him first and then you."

I was listening to all of this from the bedroom. I sat stark upright, trying to shake the sleep from my eyes and make sense of what was happening in the other room.

Then everything became crystal clear. I remembered that this guy had been visiting the house while the old man was on the road. I also remember hearing intimate noises while I was in bed so I kind of knew everything Dad was accusing them of was believable and true.

I was secretly glad she had been caught. From out of my consciousness came the thought, "Mom, how could you be showing love and affection for this guy and ignore me?" But now the events in the living room were rapidly getting out of hand.

I was afraid that somebody was about to get shot on the other side of the bedroom door. My mommy, to be exact.

While I was angry with her, I didn't want her dead. I didn't want to hear what was going on in the other room either. I wanted to be somewhere else. Anywhere else.

I remembered that during the past year Dad would take me along with him on car rides when he would stop at this bungalow. He would leave me in the car with firm instructions, "Don't get out of the car. I have a friend I have to see. Wait right here." Then he would leave for hours.

I had nothing to do and usually got bored, but didn't do anything. Finally, one day, I got out of the car and began to walk around, picking up rocks and tossing them at imaginary targets. I went up to the bungalow to try to get a peek in the window. I was not ready for the event taking place inside. I saw my father, nude, on top of this girl who was also naked. She had her legs up behind her head and he was furiously thrusting his member into her.

I had never seen anything like it. It unnerved me and caused me to run back to the car. I sat there, stunned, until he returned. My face was flush and he inquired, "What's the matter?"

I stammered, "N, n... nothing. Why?"

"Did you get out of the car?"

"Uh, yeah."

"Did you come to the window?"

"Uh-huh," I muttered shamefully.

"I thought I saw you there."

"Yeah, that was me," I admitted.

He said in a confidential tone, "You understand that there are certain things that us men keep between ourselves, right?" He nudged me in the ribs with his elbow, "Okay?"

"Yeah, sure Dad," I said, but I remember thinking, "What about Mom? Where does she fit into all of this? Am I supposed to lie to her if she asks where we were?" It was all very confusing to me.

So while Dad is making all these accusations against Mom in the living room, I realized that he had been using me as a convenient alibi while he was out with other women. "Oh, I was out running errands with the kid," he would say when we returned.

I was trying to sort all this out in my head when things

turned violent in the next room. Barry pointed the gun at Ronnie, pulled the trigger once, and misfired. In the excitement, he got his finger caught in the gun. He tried to pull it free, but instead ripped his finger almost in half, spurting blood in all directions.

In the ensuing confusion, Ronnie took the opportunity to break for the front door. He made a clean escape dashing into the alley and running for his life. Mom implored Barry, "Please, let me bandage your finger. Let me fix it." Then I could hear the sounds of him hitting her and then Mom crying. "Forget the finger," Barry spat out. "I'm going to kill you!"

Ronnie was long gone and my mom was pleading for her life. I was paralyzed with fear. "Is he going to kill her? I don't want my mother to be dead," I thought. "Oh my God, he's going to kill my mother. I'm not going to have a mother." She was screaming for her life.

It then occurred to me that if I got out of bed and went into the other room, I might be able to save her. Maybe he would be reluctant to kill her in front of me. But I was too scared to leave my bed. I didn't know what to do. Didn't know what I would say. I was terrified to get up and terrified not to. What if my mother died because I didn't get up out of bed because I was too much of a coward to go into the other room? She's out there screaming for her life and my seven-year-old brain is trying to figure out what to do. Maybe I could pacify the situation. Maybe he'd kill me too. All these cowardice issues came up for me.

I was afraid of street bullies, so that made me a coward. Both my mom and my dad thought I was sissified because I loathed violence.

Ultimately, I thought "If I don't get up now I might be responsible for my mother's death." I summoned all my courage, opened the door quietly and tenuously approached the kitchen.

The scene that greeted me was horrific. Blood was everywhere. On the counter tops, on the sink, on the walls. It looked like the Texas *Chainsaw Massacre*. Mom stood in front of the fridge with Barry's hand in hers while she tried to stem the flow of blood. Her tear-streaked face exuded pure primal fear.

And then I saw him.

His face was a blistery red. His eyes bulged a quarter-inch out of his head while sheer madness emanated from them. The bloody gun was lying on the kitchen counter next to his other hand. Both of them were spattered with blood from head to toe.

I walked into the kitchen as nonchalantly as I could. Barry raised his free hand and balled it up into a fist ready to strike mom as she bent over his wounded finger when he noticed me. He blinked a couple of times then unfolded his fist, and let her tend to a finger that seemed determined to resist any effort to stop bleeding. Blood continued dripping from underneath the rag she was using to bind the finger.

I was standing two or three feet away from them, just shifting my weight from one foot to another and waiting. There was a long, uncomfortable pause, after which things seemed to calm down. Barry just stood there fuming, smoke coming out of his ears, apparently not feeling the pain of the deep laceration. Too much adrenaline. Mom kept breaking into tears. I had never seen my mother cry. Intense hatred blazed from Barry's eyes. When he looked down at the gun, I realized that he could simply pick it up at any moment and kill her... and me, too! I didn't want to die. I didn't want my mommy to die either. There was no way to tell what might happen next. So I stood there, motionless, helpless, watching the scene develop.

In the next five minutes she managed to get the bleeding under control. I remained where I was, riveted to the floor. "You can go back to your room now," Dad stated firmly. I looked at mom and she nodded her approval. "Its OK," she said quietly. "Go back to your room."

I returned to my bed, not feeling very sleepy. I listened carefully to see if I could follow what happened next. I didn't have long to wait. Nor did I have to listen closely. The sounds were loud and definite.

He struck her with a loud, cracking smack. Then he did it again and I began to wince in pain. She began crying and he was shouting, "I know what you were doing with him."

I could hear her begging and screaming for her life. I thought, "God, now he's really going to kill her; I should go back out there but they've already told me not to. What's going to happen if I disobey them?" I concocted a scene in my head in which I went back out there and he shoots her anyway. And me, too. What's the point of going out there to first watch my mother get killed and then be shot myself? If he shoots me, my life is over.

I had all these horrible thoughts spinning in my head while the violent noises from the other room continued. She pleaded. He cursed. She begged. He hit her again. I thought I was a coward if I didn't get out of my bed. I convinced myself that I could probably save my mother's life, but I was just too scared to try.

The battle raged on both outside my bedroom door and inside me. I felt a pressure from deep inside my head. It was black and empty and invited me inside. I didn't know where the dark abyss ended, but it looked like a way out of my brutal dilemma. I passed into non-consciousness. A non-being. I remember my final thought before I went in, "I must never think of this night again as long as I live." Then it all went away. The blood. The threats. The gun. Everything. It just all went away.

When I woke up, my whole world was upside down. My little brother and I were moved into a county foster-child program. Unknown to us, our mother was under arrest for having sex with a minor and sentenced to six months in the county jail. Barry went out on the road and left no forwarding address.

We were abandoned. Eight-year-old Kenny and five year-old Ricki. In the world. Alone. In a county-funded indigent foster care home. Orphans. We had two live parents, but we were still orphans. The year 1949 was going to be a tough one for us.

Aunt Marie's

Immediately after the bloody incident in Ocean Park, Mom and Dad got a divorce. We were never told about it. He left town and dumped us into a convenient (for him) county-funded foster home. With Dad on the road and Mom in county jail, Ricki and I were on our own to deal with life the best way we could. Ricki was barely five years old, so I had to be his protector although I was only eight.

We were sent off to live with a woman we called "Aunt" Marie and her family in Alhambra, a middle-class neighborhood east of Los Angeles. Marie and Joe Costello had two children of their own, Lucille, a beautiful 16-year old who played the accordion, and Anthony, a spoiled brat about my age.

They were paid to care for kids sent to them by the county. Each ward represented money in the bank for the Costellos — and little else. The less money they spent on each kid, the more they profited for themselves. They had five kids at the time. There were two brothers, Michael and Nicky, a single girl of about seven, Denise, and my brother and me.

We weren't one big happy family though. Aunt Marie was the meanest, nastiest human being I had ever met in my short life. She had devised a lifestyle for her foster charges that would allow them to barely survive while, at the same time, putting on a brave face for the occasional visits from Mr. Cherry, the county representative assigned to monitor the home.

She saved money mostly by feeding the foster kids a steady diet of beans and oatmeal. She kept three 100-pound sacks of beans in a small space off the kitchen. At dinner time, she would boil a few cups from one of the sacks for our evening meal. Each of our five plates was offered up with a pile of beans and two pieces of day-old white bread. A container of orange colored oleomargarine was placed on our end of the table.

Meanwhile Marie and her family sat at the other end of the long table dining on excellent home-cooked Italian dishes. They had the finest cuts of meat brought to the table alongside steaming platters of pasta and vegetables. They ate heartily, while we foster kids watched with pathetic longing.

Every morning, we had mush for breakfast while Marie served her family bacon and eggs. One of the foster boys, little red-headed Nicky, hated mush. He literally could not get it down, but Marie insisted. She stood over him glaring while menacingly slapping a rolling pin in her hand. She insisted that he consume every bite, or else. It was torture to see the kid try to eat the hated bland gruel. It made for an awful start to each day. We all felt sorry for him. We wanted to help, but there was little we could do. One day when his brother Michael asked if Nicky could just skip breakfast, Marie hit Michael alongside his head as hard as she could. He never made any other requests.

Marie often used the back of her hand to elicit unquestioning obedience from her foster care charges. She would slap whoever was closest whenever she was upset. And she seemed to get upset a lot. Marie particularly enjoyed beating my brother because Ricki was a little slow and didn't always follow orders immediately. He was also the youngest and an easy target.

One day, when I was in the back yard, she began whaling on Ricki. I don't know what his particular crime was that day, but she was in a murderous state-of-mind. I was frustrated beyond belief and began crying loudly. She turned towards me and demanded, "What are you crying for? I was hitting HIM!" Through teary eyes I responded, "That's my brother, that's my brother. It's the same as if you're hitting me." She appeared bewildered and stopped hitting him.

I recognized thereafter that if she hit him I could just start crying and she would stop. It was the only defense mechanism I had, so that's what I used. Ultimately, she gave up beating him when I was around.

The hardest part of living at Aunt Marie's was trying to keep my brother's spirits up. He would come to me at night and ask, "Kenny, do we have a mommy and daddy? The other kids said we don't." I tried to reassure him. I showed him a couple of letters we had received from Dad while he was on the road. In the letters, he always said he was enclosing some spending money for us, though the money mysteriously disappeared each time. I suspected that Aunt Marie was removing it from the envelopes. I said, "Don't listen to them. They don't know anything. Mom and Dad will come back to get us, you'll see." He seemed reassured but said, "I wish it could be soon. I hate it here."

All the foster kids were required to stay in the back yard when we were not in school. Under no circumstances were we permitted in the house with the Costello family. It was a spacious back yard dominated by two large trees, one apricot and the other peach. Both produced copious amounts of delicious fruit. The trees grew hundreds of the best peaches and apricots I had ever tasted. Despite Marie's dire warnings that if any of us so much "touched one piece of fruit" we would "regret it for months to come," the temptation was too great.

We plotted a fruit raid with military precision. One of us would pretend to play near the house and keep an eye out for Marie. If she appeared, the spy would say loudly, "Oh, hi Aunt Marie! Do you need some help in the house?"

As soon as we heard the warning, we would swallow whole whatever we had in our hands. Failure to do so would lead to unthinkable consequences. We all lived in terror of being discovered. We knew the type of beating that would await anyone caught.

Meanwhile, the rest of the Costello family lived a good life. Lucille received piano, accordion, and singing lessons. Every night we could hear her practicing from the living room, a place we were forbidden to enter.

Uncle Joe went to work and left the running of the house to his wife. He brought home enough money to pay the bills and put great food on the table. Anthony was the pampered prince of the house who never had to do anything. He often refused to finish his food and we all waited 'til the end of the meal when we could clear the dishes and eat his leftovers.

Doing the dishes and scrubbing pots and pans was our daily assignment. Because I could never get enough to eat, I would snag a slice of bread while at the kitchen sink and shove the whole thing in my mouth at once to avoid discovery.

One night, Marie burst into the kitchen unexpectedly just

as I had placed a piece of pilfered bread in my mouth. It got caught in my throat and I began to turn red. "What's the matter with him?" she demanded. One of the other kids answered, "Oh, he's OK. He just needs a drink of water." He poured me a big glass of tap water which I used to pass the doughy bread past my esophagus.

Once I created an uncomfortable scene in the house when I brought home an outstanding report card. Joe looked at my grades and said to Anthony, "Look how well this kid does. How come you don't get grades like that?" His son simply shrugged his shoulders. "I don't like school. Kenny is a loser who sucks up to the teachers."

When it was time for a visit from the county supervisor to check up on us, Marie pulled us aside and warned us in severe terms, "Mr. Cherry is coming today. You had better tell him everything is fine here, or you'll be sorry." I knew she was referring to the beatings she had been administering to my brother. I wanted to tell Mr. Cherry, but I was afraid of the consequences, so I said nothing when he arrived. I was worried that she would deny everything we protested, and he would believe her. I couldn't take that chance.

Somehow we got through that year. Barry came off the road, Mom got out of jail, and they remarried. They came to retrieve us at Aunt Marie's and took us to our new home in the West Adams district of L.A.

Alsace Avenue

Our move into the modest house at 2501 Alsace Avenue in a middle-class neighborhood marked the first time in my nine years that we had a regular life. It was a two-bedroom home with a living room and dining area, with a large fenced yard in back. Rent was $75 a month. Our landlord was a man named Mr. Wells, who was about to take an extended trip to the Philippines. Mom looked like an ordinary housewife and we looked like normal people.

It was a mixed neighborhood with a few Jewish families, many WASP families, along with some Mexican families and some blacks. It was about as diversified as any L.A. neighborhood could get. Kids were left free to roam the area on their bicycles, play ball in the street, or hang out in the school yard. There were no gangs, no graffiti, and no homeless; only ordinary working-class people going about the daily business of living. Dad goes to work, Mom stays at home and the kids go to school.

I had a free-rein over my own life. My brother was now in school too, so I had almost no responsibilities tending to him. I left the house when I wanted to. I came home when I wanted to. I put myself to bed at night. Even though I had such unrestricted freedom, I continued to get good grades in school, worked at selling papers after school, and generally showed good judgment about handling my affairs. I was doing what a responsible child ought to do. Such a good boy!

But there were things going on in the house which I could not fathom. Dad's friends were coming and going at all hours of the day and throughout the night. Mysterious meetings in the bedroom. Strange smells emanating from the bathroom. I didn't know what any of it was about and I really didn't care. No one ever asked me how my life was going, what was happening in school, or if I was doing my homework. In fact, nobody ever asked me anything. I came and went as I pleased and tucked myself in for the night when I wanted to.

As normal as we seemed though, there were several things we didn't have in the house: family discussions, books or other reading materials, or anything that would challenge one to think. We shared our living space, but existed in separate and distinct worlds.

I had a job selling newspapers after school. I had to work because my parents never gave me any money. The only way I had to get cash was to earn it. I sold daily papers on the corner of Adams and Alsace, or Adams and La Brea, or Adams and Crenshaw. I would report to work everyday after school and spend two or three hours in traffic peddling papers.

In those days, there were several morning newspapers and an afternoon paper — the *Herald Express*, the *Mirror*, the *L.A. Times*, the *L.A. Daily News*, and the *L.A. Examiner*. I sold them all. The afternoon papers were favored by the Hollywood Park crowd looking for the horse race results. I was dedicated to the job and I made money. I saved my pennies, nickels, and dimes. I always had my own little stash. I was a budding entrepreneur.

I attended Cienega grammar school, which was only a few blocks from our house. One of my teachers was Mrs. Kramer, aunt of the tennis star Jack Kramer. She was the first "almost celebrity" I ever met. I also met Harry Thompson, a large black man who owned a gas station and played football for the L.A. Rams.

I did well in school once again. It seemed easy for me and I couldn't understand why some of the students didn't get the daily lessons even after they were repeated several times. I became restless and disruptive. I made jokes and shot rubber bands across the room. I was loud and annoying. I was bored.

One day, the school called my parents in. Of course, my dad never showed up for anything, so my mom went with me to the meeting. The principal said, "Mrs. Kahn, we have to make some changes in your son's education. He absorbs everything quite rapidly. He soaks up the lessons then proceeds to disturb the entire class. He needs more of a challenge."

Mom took all of this in as though the principal had been speaking Greek. "So you're telling me he's been bad?" she inquired. "You're not going to throw him out of school are you?" The principal smiled and said, "No. Nothing like that!

We just have to find some way to keep your son interested in class. I have discussed it with the other teachers and we think Kenny should be in the sixth grade next year."

"SIXTH GRADE!" Faye repeated incredulously. "He's only in THIRD GRADE now! If you put him in the sixth grade he'll be graduating to junior high in a year. That seems pretty fast."

The principal responded, "It's really up to you. You can go home and discuss it with your family and let me know. He really has an exceptional learning ability. You should consider maximizing it."

Mom was irritated. "You know I have better things to do than be called into the principal's office at your school," she said to me on the way home. "Why can't you behave yourself? What's your problem?"

I explained, "They teach us real simple stuff and then repeat it about a billion times. I have to do something to keep myself occupied. I guess I fool around quite a bit."

She finally told me that I should make the final decision myself. That decision was a difficult one to make. I thought about being younger and physically less developed than my classmates. Leaping three grades sounded bad. My favorite thing in life was playing ball. I had a great competitive spirit, but not great athletic skills. I was keeping up with my classmates on the basketball court, but just barely. I couldn't imagine where I would fit in with much older boys. I figured I'd get smashed. I was, as my high school football coach later noted, 'small but slow.'

I finally decided they could skip me one year, from the third grade to the fifth. It worked out better in class because I was not quite as bored, but I was not as physically developed as the other kids and got pushed around a bit.

The Family Business

On the eve of my tenth birthday my dad came to me and said, "It's time for you to hit the road. Would you like to come with me to the California State Fair in Sacramento?" He added, "You can make some good 'scratch' there."

It all sounded good to me, especially the money part. I had been earning between seventy-five cents and a dollar pushing newspapers in traffic for three hours a day after school. But this was a chance to make some REAL money. Plus going to the state capitol with my dad sounded exciting. "Sure," I said, and that was it. I was excited to embark on a brand new chapter in my young life.

My first lesson learned was the city of Sacramento in the summer is the hottest place this side of hell. I could barely breathe when I got off the train from L.A., two days before the fair started. Barry checked us into the Equipoise Hotel where the carnies stayed. He rented us a stuffy room with a useless, noisy ceiling fan. This was to be our home for the next three weeks.

He then took me to an air-conditioned movie theatre while he went back to the Equipoise where his buddies were engaged in non-stop gambling in the Card Room. I didn't mind being left alone. The cool, darkened theatre offered the only relief from the stifling heat. When the flick ended, I simply shifted to the next movie house down the street. During the next two days, I saw every movie in town – twice. I must have eaten ten gallons of popcorn.

On the Fair's opening day, Dad drove us to the sprawling state fairgrounds to introduce me to my new bosses. He chose the entrance nearest the rides and games of the carnival midway. We parked and walked to the gate where the attendant asked for our tickets. "We're *with it*," Barry said to him and the guy waved us through.

"How did you do that?" I asked as we entered the fairgrounds. He replied, "When you're working on the show as a carny, you just crack that you're 'with it.' Whenever you come onto the lot, you just say those words and he'll let you in. You don't need any badges or passes."

I was impressed. I had never had that kind of power. Being

a kid, I never would have guessed that there were secret codes that only insiders recognized. I also didn't know it at the time that there were many more insider secrets to come. Dad warned, "You're never to tell anyone about anything you learn on the carnival lot. Especially the marks. You never wake up a sucker."

Dad steered me onto the midway where there were dozens of joints lining both sides of the grounds. It appeared as though every imaginable game of chance was represented: ball games, dart games, coin tosses, wheels of fortune and more. They were interspersed between kiddie rides, cotton-candy stands, and thrill rides. Dad explained that the games were known as "joints" and the people who ran them as "agents." In the early morning hours, the carnies were opening up the joints, or 'springing' them as they called it, preparing for the day. Other than a few kids, there were no customers or "marks" to be seen this early.

Dad introduced me to the two young women who would become my bosses for the duration of the fair. They were sisters, Joni and Loraine, and they couldn't have been more than 17 or 18 years of age. Both were attractive and energetic. Joni, the shorter, cuter of the two, explained what my job would be.

The front of their joint faced the midway and appeared to be a simple game of throwing darts at balloons, although when we arrived there were no balloons to be seen, only empty hooks on a wall.

Loraine, the taller of the two girls, hopped over the counter and approached the blank wall. She pushed one side of the wall and it moved, rotating 180 degrees, exposing an identical set of hooks on the other side. Behind the wall was a small, cramped space, rather dark except for a single bare light bulb. The floor was stacked with several large cardboard boxes holding new balloons, an air machine, and a lone stool. That was for me.

"Your job is to inflate the balloons, tie them up, and place them on the hooks on the wall. As soon as we need more balloons out front, we rotate the wall where you will have hooked a whole new wall full of freshly-inflated balloons. Once we spin around the wall, you have to get busy filling the used side with a new batch. Got it?"

They showed me how to use the air compressor and tie a knot in the balloon. Then I was left alone in the darkened space, three feet by twelve feet. It was hot and stuffy. I was already rather suspicious about how great this job was going to be. But it didn't matter; I was there and I had no choice.

I began work immediately. The only time I saw daylight was when one of the girls turned the wall for a new set of balloons or when they gave me a short break. Other than that, I sat in the dank quarters for fifteen hours a day. It was tedious, repetitive, and sweaty work. The only thing that kept me going was the thought of the reward, one dollar per hour. The magnificent total of fifteen dollars per day, in cash, paid at the end of each day.

We lived a brutal work schedule. The rides and games shut down at midnight. Then Dad and I joined the other carnies for a late night breakfast before returning to the hotel to collapse at 2:00 a.m. Then I was awakened at 7:00 a.m. to return to the fairgrounds for another fifteen hour shift. I learned later that carnivals are normally closed during the day on weekdays, playing from sunset 'til midnight. Full days were worked on weekends only. But State Fairs like this one are different. They are full blown marathons from day one to their closing day.

The only truly enjoyable times from my first "carny" experience were the breaks I had in which I got to explore the other parts of the fairgrounds and the midnight breakfasts with the older guys.

They taught me how to "roll" a restaurant. Although there were as many as fifteen of us at a table, we all requested separate checks. When it was time to leave, each carny would give his check to one guy to pay. Then everyone would leave a nice tip and head to the parking lot.

Finally, the guy with the checks goes to the cashier and pays...but only his own check. All the rest of the checks remain in his pocket. Meanwhile, everyone else has split. Scam completed. The waitress doesn't notice what's going on because there is a large tip on the table. Meanwhile, the guy with the checks is apparently paying at the cash register, and nobody notices the unpaid bills until all the carnies are long gone. If someone does wake up, the guy at the counter has paid HIS bill and is in the clear. Some carnies bragged they had not paid a restaurant bill in years.

The Pitch

The following year, my carny education began in earnest when Dad and I joined a traveling carnival. This time, I got a job working at the "dime pitch." This joint involved a large central platform such that marks had four sides from which to play.

The game seemed easy on the surface. The wooden platform occupied the center of the interior space. On the platform were situated dozens of large plush toy animals, either teddy bears or poodles, each worth about $25 at the local toy store. A shallow glass plate was placed on the head of each animal. If a player landed a coin in the dish, the prize was the toy directly under it. A simple proposition. Just land a dime on a dish and win an expensive cuddly reward for your sweetie.

Then I learned the "G" or "gaff" on the joint. Every day before opening, the employees would coat each dish with a special wax that made the surface of the plate super slippery. The substance worked so well, it was nearly impossible to land a coin on the dish even from a couple of inches away. To make extra certain there were no lucky accidents, each plate was tilted imperceptibly inward, away from the players to assure maximum protection from the occasional winning toss. Out of thousands of dimes pitched, maybe just one or two chance coins would ever produce a winner.

My job was to "call" marks to the joint and encourage them to play. I also had to make change, which I soon discovered was an art in itself. When someone gave you a bill, you didn't necessarily have to return ALL the change. I learned that people were easily distracted by the excitement of the moment. The busy midway was crowded with partying patrons, noisy thrill rides, candy apple stands, and hot dogs on sticks. Add to that the hope of winning a highly desirable prize for your best girl made the careful counting of your change unimportant. Carnies were keenly aware of how to take advantage of these conditions.

I soon discovered that I could make more money from short changing people than I could from my paltry salary. I was taught to deal with the situation where I got caught by saying, "Sorry, my fault. Here's the rest of your change." I reckoned I averaged between $20 and $40 extra a day.

The summer of 1952 was my first full-time job as part of a traveling carnival. I was eleven and already learning the ropes at an accelerated rate. Dad had switched from working with the West Coast Shows that played throughout the Pacific Northwest to the Sutton Shows, which spent the entire season in the state of Utah. Barry was on good terms with the show owner, Pete Sutton, who felt we could do well on the road with his show. I didn't know it at the time, but the real reason was that Sutton allowed certain highly illegal games that wouldn't have been permitted on the more urban West Coast Shows.

These high-powered "games of chance" were called "Flat Stores," and were designed to reap huge harvests of dollars from well-heeled, unsuspecting marks. They were so blatantly unfair, the carnival had to pay off the local cops just to set them up. They were operated by a sophisticated corps of elite thieves known as "Flatties."

It took years of training to master the scam, and only the top carnies had cultivated the art. Of these, Dad was widely recognized as one of the best.

As I moved up the carny ladder of success, I was given increasingly advanced opportunities to make money. These positions required different job skills, but were more financially rewarding.

I was put to work in the milk-bottle joint. A relatively simple game, the object was to throw a ball at three silver bottles stacked up – two on the bottom supporting one on top – and knock all three over with a single shot. The mark stood behind a low counter about 15 feet from the bottles and paid 25 cents a shot. "Knock over the bottles and win your choice of any prize in the house," I cried out to passersby on the midway.

What I didn't say was that the bottles that appeared to be identical were actually quite different. Two of them were hollow and weighed about eight ounces. The third one was filled with cement and weighed nearly eight *pounds*. When I wanted to demonstrate how easy it was to win, I'd put the heavy bottle on top and pitch a ball at them. Any contact, however slight, would cause all the bottles to fall. It didn't matter where I struck them. Just lightly grazing the heavy bottle with the ball would do the trick.

But when I didn't want the bottles to tip over, all I had to do was place the heavy one on the bottom, slightly in front of the others. You could hit that baby with a major league fastball and it would just slide backwards a few inches. If you hit it directly, the ball would come flying back at you faster than you threw it, nearly decapitating any players around you. Every once in awhile, a perfect shot would get all three of them, but that was rare.

My pay was equal to one-third of all the money I collected during the day. Since the owner had to pay for the rental of the space, replace any lost prizes, and pay for the costs of trucking everything from town-to-town, he kept two-thirds of the take. That arrangement seemed fair at first, until my dad introduced me to the concept of the "H.O.," meaning "Hold Out," which was the carny's version of fair. Also known as "Oats," it meant simply that you didn't turn in all the money in your apron. It was a time-tested practice at the carnival and apparently everyone did it. There were two unspoken rules: one, don't get caught. And two, don't take more than 25% of the total take.

Using those guidelines, I learned how to do quite well. By combining the three inside carny techniques of rigging the game, short-changing, and Oats, I made more money than I'd ever seen before. First you steal from unsuspecting marks, then short-change them, then steal from your boss, a nifty program for sure. Follow that with not paying for restaurant tabs and you can make a bundle on the road.

Deadwood

Dad and I broke away from the Sutton shows for a week that summer to play a big celebration in a small town two states away. From Salt Lake City, we drove across the southern part of Wyoming to reach the Black Hills of South Dakota. It was a long drive and we passed the time singing songs and telling jokes. Dad also used the opportunity to school me in the fine art of analyzing marks. While he was no psychologist, he taught me how to read body language, judge how much money a guy was willing to spend, and when to cool him out and end the play. We were traveling with his old running partner, Leo "the Lion" Schroeder.

This carnival set up right on the streets in Deadwood, South Dakota. We were there for a celebration known as the "Days of 76" that marked the famous silver rush of that year a century ago. The dinky town of 5,000 people swelled to 20,000 – 30,000 during the event. It was a true "Wild West" happening.

The local hotels and motels were filled to overflowing with real and wannabe cowboys. The bars were hopping from early morning to late night, serving revelers who liked to live life on the edge. Street fights were common. It was not unusual to see a body come flying through the swinging doors of a saloon. Six-guns were worn openly in public.

Each day, there was a theatrical reproduction of the shooting of Wild Bill Hickok, who died of a gunshot wound in Deadwood. An argument would suddenly break out amongst a group of cowboys playing cards at a poker table. Wild Bill, holding aces and eights, known from that day forward as the "Dead Man's Hand," was shot at the end of the argument. The killer then bolted for the front door and into the street, chased by an informal posse. He was soon caught, tried on a makeshift platform, and sentenced to hang. To me, it seemed like the real Wild West, not a recreation.

I had a room in a rickety old wooden hotel which overlooked the main street of town. I was working the rifle shoot, a game that used .22 rifles loaded with real ammunition. The idea was to shoot at a paper card with a red dot on it. The card was situated at the end of a six foot steel tube and the player had three shots to attempt to completely blow away the dot to win a prize.

Despite the fact that many of the cowboys were excellent shots, nobody ever won a prize. The gaff was that the cards were designed in such a way that even if the three shots were clustered perfectly, part of the dot could not be blown away. It was made to simply fold over behind the card. When I pulled the card forward to show it to the customer as proof of his bad aim, I could reach behind it and expose a tiny bit of red. Even when it appeared to be a clean winner, I had a magnifying glass to highlight the miniscule fragments of red still remaining. Some of the cowboy marks would go ballistic when that happened.

Meanwhile, Dad and his buddy Leo had gotten themselves caught up in a major jackpot. They had beaten a guy out of seven hundred bucks. Although the mark didn't know how, he knew that the game was crooked and that his money had been stolen. He left the midway but returned in an hour with a couple of his friends looking for the two carnival thieves. They were rough and tumble dudes who probably didn't need the pistols they had tucked into their waistbands to do serious damage.

Dad and Leo were pretty tough customers themselves, but well beyond their prime. A carny soon learns that discretion is often the better part of valor. In this case, not being present for their return seemed like a good idea. These marks were not only upset, but out for blood.

Barry was the first to spot the three of them heading down the crowded midway towards their joint. He gave Leo the high sign, and the two of them quickly slipped under the flap of the tent in back. It was an escape route they had used successfully in the past. But this time it didn't work. One of the mark's buddies had stationed himself at the rear and yelled out, "Hey, they're back here!"

The two carnies instantly returned inside the tent. When they saw the two marks in front run to the back where their friend was yelling, they profited from the opportunity to hop over the front counter and disappear into the crowd. As they passed me, Dad called out, "You're on your own. We'll catch up with you in Provo." But he didn't bother to say how I was to get to Provo. I was left to figure that out myself.

The three cowboys returned to the midway, spotted the culprits running away in the distance, and began chasing them. Dad and Leo were able to get away, but the cowboys didn't give up, patrolling the carnival lot for hours until closing. They even returned at 6:00 a.m. the next day. Luckily, they didn't know that I was Barry's kid, so I continued to work the rest of the fair. I had to make money for both of us that week. It was also the first time in my life that I had ever been alone. It was somewhat frightening. I was 11 years old and living on the main street of Deadwood, South Dakota in a seedy old hotel. I worked all day and most of the night. The place was packed. The fairgrounds were teeming with partygoers, yelling and shouting and having a general all-around good time.

Since the carnival was set up on Main Street, you could wander off the midway and find yourself right in town. It didn't really matter where you were because the party carried on everywhere.

Because we had jumped from our regular show to play Deadwood, I didn't know any of the other carnies. Barry didn't know any of them either and had warned me to stay away from them, lest I get cheated. So I spent the week keeping my own company. There were probably not a lot of 11-year old kids living on their own and walking around with a few hundred dollars in their pocket. I realized then that I could maintain myself at the carnival.

I was actually doing more than maintaining myself. I was saving money. I treated myself to the finest steak dinners. I came and went as I pleased. I fantasized what life might be like if I were older and could take part in the festivities going on around me. But mainly I worked. I toiled long, hard hours. At the end of the day, I was exhausted and just wanted to collapse. Unfortunately, resting is not an option during the "Days of '76" celebrations. The whoopin' 'n' hollerin' went on 'til dawn. I didn't get much sleep that week.

One night after work, I bumped into a cute little Gypsy girl named Gina. I had seen her by the "mitt camp," the name that carnies gave to the Gypsies who travel with the show.

The term "mitt" referred to the palm readings the Gypsies peddled. They lived and worked together as a separate group within the carnival.

I had only recently begun to have an interest in girls. I never had much use for them when I was younger, but now they somehow seemed more interesting, and Gina was very, very cute.

She had smiled at me whenever we passed each other at the carnival. For days, I didn't know what to do with her, so I did nothing. Then one day during a break, I bumped into her at the snow cone stand. She was in line ahead of me. I said "Hi," and asked her if I could buy her a snow cone. She said, "No thanks." I tried again, "How about a ride on the Ferris wheel. I can get us on." She said, "I have to get back, but if you can get us on immediately, I'll go." We went directly to the wheel where I asked the ride boy, Jerry, to let us on first. He looked at Gina and smiled lasciviously. "Yeah, sure. I understand completely."

He moved us to the front of the line and opened the door of the next available car for us. We got in and sat down in the swinging bucket seat. Jerry pulled the metal bar down to secure us. It was very warm and cozy. I liked it. She seemed like she did too. She snuggled against me as the wheel began to lift us up above the midway. Somehow I found myself holding hands with her, and my heart began to beat a million miles an hour.

The wheel steadily propelled us up to the very top where we had a view of the town and surrounding countryside. The scenery was spectacular, or maybe it was the fact that I was sitting with a beautiful Gypsy princess who was allowing me to hold her hand. Either way it was the highlight of my week.

We ran into each other "accidentally" several times during the following days. We eventually consummated our relationship with a kiss on a trip through the Tunnel of Love. Though the ride only lasted two minutes, we made the most of it. My interest in girls was growing by leaps and bounds.

Hanky-Panks, Alibis & Flat Stores

I had started out on the lowest rung of the carnival operator's hierarchy. I didn't know it at the time, but I was being groomed, or "turned out," by my Dad.

There is a clearly defined ladder of employment on the midway. At the very bottom were the "ruffies," the grease-stained, foul-mouthed manual laborers whose efforts made it possible for the carnival to operate, move, and mechanically function. They were the movers and packers who loaded the show trucks with the heavy metal components, tents and tools, and everything else the show needed to set up operations. They were the grease-monkeys who repaired the rides when they broke down. On closing day, they worked until the early morning hours packing and stowing gear. Then they drove the trucks a couple of hundred miles to the next spot, unloaded the trucks, and set up the entire midway. Only then were they allowed to sleep.

They were looked on as lower than scum by the carnies, not even worthy of being called "carnies." They were low-life slime balls with no ability to steal money from unsuspecting marks, therefore not even worth recognizing. They were paid so little that they could not afford even the lowest-priced room in a flea-bag hotel. They slept on a cot inside one of the tents instead. There were no bathroom facilities or showers other than the public restrooms which were used by hundreds of fairgoers every day. Ruffies washed up in the cold water sinks once or twice a week. I never knew any one of them to launder their clothes.

They were also counted on to be the unofficial security for the show. Whenever some local tough punks wanted to start trouble, all we had to do was call out, "Hey Rube." The ruffies would come running to do battle.

Marks who were troublemakers were called "rangs," an epithet drawn from the word "orangutans." They were usually young guys who had too much to drink and wanted to beat someone up to get even for a friend who had been fleeced out of a bunch of money. More than getting the money back, they preferred to start a fight. It was almost always a mistake, for them.

The ruffies who came out to meet them liked nothing better than a good fight. Armed with tire irons, wrenches, and knives they knew how to handle the toughest situations.

The biggest, baddest ruffie on the West Coast Shows was a Hawaiian guy called Pineapple. He could single-handedly whip any six guys alive. He was maybe five-foot six — in both directions. He looked like he could play nose tackle for the Green Bay Packers. He was bad to the bone. Alone, he could handle most disturbances. He was the toughest-looking guy I had ever seen. More than once, just the sight of the guy was enough to cool out the meanest, nastiest drunks.

Dad told me to steer clear of the ruffies. Never make friends with them. In fact, never rap with them or even make friendly gestures. They weren't real carnies and deserved only scorn. Except when they were needed to fight, of course. Then we were all buddies.

Real carnies were called "agents," smooth-talking con-artists who were well versed in the skills of separating marks from their money.

At the lowest rung of agent's joints were the "Hanky Panks," which depended on high volume. They were designed to make a little money from a lot of people. These were your typical carnival games where you threw balls at bottles, darts at balloons, or coins at a dish. If marks were lucky, it was possible for them to win small prizes like whistles or Chinese finger traps. Some of the hanky joints advertised "a prize every time," but these were nearly worthless trophies, known as "slum." They were the staple of the hanky's business. Marks could only win a larger prize after spending enough money to pay for it three times over.

Hankies often used "shills" or "sticks" to increase their business. A shill is a carnival employee who pretends to be a mark who suddenly wins a large prize. The agent makes a great, noisy hoopla of handing out the plush bears or poodles to the shill, who then pretends like he had just won big. "Hey, there goes another one! That's the fifth winner in the last hour, folks," the agent calls out loudly. The passing crowd stops to take notice and some of them reach for their wallets. The shill beams with joy at his new acquisition and holds it up for all to see before strutting off with his treasure. Then he makes his way around the midway where he deposits the toy under the back flap of the joint where it came from.

My little brother, Ricki, was taught to be a shill. He won large prizes all day long and earned plenty of pocket money for his acting skills.

The first thing you learn as a new agent is how to "call" fairgoers who stroll past your joint. That's how you get the attention of potential marks. There are a number of ways to perfect the call. It often depends on who the mark is. Young people are your primary target; the younger, the better. Some agents made their money just by playing to kids.

Barry showed me how to pry a sticky quarter from the hand of a kid clutching a half-eaten stick of cotton candy. He demonstrated a direct technique that avoided any sales pitch, by simply grabbing the child's fingers and prying the coin loose. Once you had the money in your hand it was much easier to convince the kid to play the game. With small children, this approach worked exceedingly well.

One slow Saturday afternoon, I was trying to convince a six-year old to give me his 25 cents to throw a ball. The kid was hemming and hawing and fidgeting with the quarter held tightly in his candy-apple stained fingers. I had already spent fifteen minutes trying to convince the kid to give the game a try. He wouldn't commit, preferring instead to look from side to side at other joints competing for his attention and money.

Barry showed up just at that time and sized up the situation. He winked at me and said, "Pay attention." He went directly up to the kid and forcibly removed the quarter from his tiny hand and stuck a ball in its place. "Throw it," he commanded. The kid looked confused, but then threw the ball. It missed everything. "Try it again," Barry prodded. The kid shrugged, "I don't have any more money." Barry shrugged to the kid, "Too bad."

His young eyes filled with tears as he turned and dejectedly headed down the midway. Barry winked and gave me the high sign with his thumb and forefinger. "That's how *you* get the cash and not the guy in the next joint. Someone's gonna get the kid's money. It might as well be you."

Another time, I was struggling with a youngster who refused to fork over his allowance. He insisted that he was broke. Dad arrived just in time to teach me another lesson. He bent down till his head was even with the kid's face, then plunged his hand into the kid's pocket, quickly extracting any money. Triumphantly, Barry exclaimed, "Well, look what I found here." He waved a dollar bill, then placed a ball in the youngster's hand. "Throw it," he insisted. When the child missed, Barry handed him another ball. "Try it again." He proceeded to coerce the kid into throwing four balls, spending his whole dollar. When it was over Barry said, "Sorry, you lose. Better luck next time." The kid looked stunned. Barry gently said goodbye and pushed him out into the midway.

He confided in me, "That's how you play this joint. You gotta make the decision for the little marks. You take charge. Once you have the money in your hand, just keep feeding them balls 'til they're broke."

Later that night, he also showed me how to deal with reluctant adults. Nothing helped business better than encouraging two young men to try to show off for their girlfriends. Barry started up a steady stream of inciting chatter. He got two guys with their girls to compete against each other. "Don't let your buddy show you up," he harangued one guy. "Show him who's boss. It only takes one good one to make up for all the bad ones. C'mon. Try it," he challenged the other.

Each guy handed him a ten dollar bill. Instead of handing the change back to the players, he laid it on the counter. As the marks fired the balls, Barry slowly helped himself to bits of the remaining cash. Neither guy thought to check if Dad was keeping an accurate account of affairs. Suddenly the change was all gone and Barry pointed to the bare counter, "You need another quarter to keep playing, fellas." Both players looked a bit startled but, fearing being perceived as cheap by their girls, they each produced another ten smackers. Their cash went just as fast as the first time, yet they won nothing. They finally gave up and ambled off in embarrassment.

By the time the two chumps were departing, a large group

had gathered to watch the competition. Before the crowd had a chance to disperse, Barry called out to onlookers, "O.K. who's next?" He worked them with precision, dragging onlookers physically from the back of the crowd to the counter where he shamed them into giving the game a try.

Soon others were lining up behind them, money in hand, ready and anxious to play. He had created what carnies call a "tip," a large number of players happily waiting to play the next game. At this point, no salesmanship is necessary. Just collect the money as quickly as possible and keep the games going rapidly.

This tip lasted for over an hour and we cleaned up. It was fun. I had never made so much money in such a short time in my life. The action was so fast and furious, it wasn't even necessary to shortchange the marks.

The Alibi

Certain carnival games were able to be controlled by the agent who had a gaff or some physical device that he could activate, thereby dictating the outcome of the game. To marks, these games appeared to be quite easy to win, but they were completely rigged. The two I learned to turn out on were the "buckets" and the "six-cat."

The buckets were simply open mesh fruit baskets attached to a frame and angled slightly downward. The idea was to land three balls in the basket and not have them bounce out. The gaff was that any ball will bounce out every time unless the operator left another ball in the bottom of the basket. If there was a ball already in the basket when the mark tossed his ball, the inside one caused the thrown one to deaden and not bounce out. In this way, the operator could make it appear that it was possible to win. He could let the mark have a free practice shot that proved how easy it was to get the ball to stay in the basket.

When you had such complete control of a game, the possibilities were endless. You could offer multiple prizes as an inducement. You could offer to buy them back for outrageous prices, then keep the mark going.

Ultimately, the key to financial success was that the agent had to say something to the mark to encourage him to keep playing. He had to create a line of chatter that is a combination of wit, flattery, and creative explanations for why the player was able to land a ball in the basket successfully every time, except when he went to shoot for prizes. Thus, the alibi.

I was sent to apprentice with "Buckets Brownie," the leading legendary alibi agent who had more than 40 years of experience. A gnarled gnome of a man, reminiscent of Burgess Meredith in Rocky, Brownie worked his joint to perfection. With his slouch hat tilted rakishly on his head, he could mesmerize just about any unlucky victim, unload his wallet, and still leave the mark laughing.

He was so entertaining and amusing, while manipulating the game both physically and psychologically, that he resembled a close-up magician doing card tricks. It was never a straight-forward sell. He would ask personal questions of the mark. Brownie soon knew his name, his marital status and which sports team he follows. He used all this information to distract and play with the mark while taking his money, throwing out alibis along the way. He and his marks always became instant best friends.

But sometimes a mark would wake up and realize he'd been cheated. Anger often ensued, though it usually stopped short of getting physical. "Buckets Brownie" could cool out the hottest victim. He had about fifteen different techniques he used. He got philosophical, "Hey, you can't win 'em all," he would chide. Or he'd make a joke, "Hey Joe, I bet your wife doesn't complain about you missing so much."

If absolutely necessary, Buckets would relent and give the mark a nice prize to take with him. Returning money was known as a "KB," a kickback. It was absolutely the worst thing that could happen to a play. The carny's ever-present nightmare was taking off a big score, but then having to KB it. That was going from the highest high to the lowest low in a matter of minutes. So cooling out marks was a major part of Alibi 101. *Never ever return money* was the ruling mantra.

While working as an apprentice to Brownie, I flubbed up many times, causing him to curse at me when no one else was around. He made me feel like an idiot. Once I nearly got us "sloughed" or closed down because of a particularly inept play. The mark woke up to the scam and threatened to call the police. Only Brownie's intervention saved the day. Unfortunately we had to KB all the money and give up a half dozen valuable prizes as well.

Brownie blamed me and complained loudly to my old man who was forced to cough up the dough and beg Brownie not to fire me. Eventually, the grizzled carny relented and permitted me to return to work. Although Dad never physically punished me, he found a hundred ways to needle me about my transgressions. The mental whipping went on for weeks. I was shattered, but vowed to study hard and learn everything my tutor had to offer.

The Six-Cat

The six-cat was a completely different type of alibi joint. When I was working a hanky-pank, I liked to study the intricate workings of the game. Every time I got a break, I would hang around the well-designed joint with its four-foot high counter blocking any view of the interior except the walls of the tent which were bedecked with fine prizes and the cats, themselves happily ensconced on their perch.

The joint looked like a cinch to win. Six large dolls with painted 'happy cat' faces stood on a platform about five feet off the ground and about four feet from the spot the mark was to throw a ball in an attempt to knock the cat off its perch. The closeness of the target and the large size of the cats made it appear almost too easy.

Despite being called the six-cat, the object of the game was simply to knock three of the cats off the rack and into the net below using three fat softballs. But if any cat was knocked down but did not fall into the net below, you lost.

I watched the play from a corner of the counter, which was about five feet from the joint. I could see the carnies on an elevated platform on the other side of the counter.

Two agents ran the joint. One was "No-Sox" Bob, a wannabe hipster in his mid-twenties who was just breaking in after several seasons of working the hankies. He was always dressed in mismatched plaid slacks and a checkered shirt. The other was old Shorty, who had run the six-cat for over thirty years. The two of them operated differently, but both made good money.

Shorty was a good-humored, happy-go-lucky, wizened old man who had long ago realized that he would live out his days on a carnival lot. He accepted it with conviviality. He lived for pilfering money semi-legally. He was a die-hard thief and reveled in it. He had cultivated the art of stealing and having the suckers love him nonetheless. He put on a show that was worth paying to see.

I watched often and for long periods of time, studying the game. I desperately wanted to know how it worked. How could a mark knock two cats off the rack while the third one would just lay down flat on the shelf? It was a mystery I couldn't figure out.

I tried listening carefully to what Shorty told the marks after they kept scoring two out of three. He offered things like, "You threw too hard," or "You have to hit him directly on his red nose, just right," or "That one was off to the side."

After a few more misses, Shorty would lean towards the mark's ear and say in a confidential tone, "I'm not supposed to do this, but you seem like a nice guy, so just knock off two with two balls and you win your choice of any of these fine prizes." He pointed to a portable stereo system mounted on a shelf, an expensive Rolex watch, fine cutlery sets as well as the standard plush Pandas and Poodles. This joint was well stocked with more seductive prizes than I had ever seen in any of the hankies. Some of it was really neat shit.

When the mark agreed to play again, Shorty nonchalantly added, "Of course, it'll cost you a dollar to play now instead of fifty cents."

Although Shorty had lightened the mark's load to having to knock only two cats off the shelf, this time the unsuspecting player would invariably knock only one cat off. The other kept getting hung up on the shelf. How did this happen? Shorty would offer the guy more theories. "Ya' hit it too soft. A little low, as well. Try it again. Remember one good one makes up for all the bad ones. That'll be another dollar."

After a few more misses, Shorty resorted to his confidential tone once again. "My boss would kill me if he knew I was doing this, but I'll tell you what, just knock down one cat and you'll win. Of course, I have to charge you five dollars for that game."

The mark agreed, and slipped him a twenty, which Shorty didn't bother to change. The guy then pitched the single ball. It hit the cat squarely on the nose. The cat fell backwards, but then got caught on the rack. A loser, but Shorty showed the guy some pity. "Just off to the right. Try it again." The guy agreed, but once again, it's another loser. Then another, and another, until the entire twenty was burned.

The mark finally got disgusted and angry. "I don't get it. There's something strange about this game. At first, it was easy for me to knock off two cats. Now I can't even knock off one. And I'm spending five bucks a shot. I'm out twenty-five bucks."

Shorty still doesn't give up. Ever helpful, he suggests, "Look I'll tell you what I'll do. I'm taking these twenty-five smackers you spent and putting them in this cigar box." He extracted a box from under the counter and dropped the bills in it. "When you win now, I'll give you the prize *and* the contents of the cigar box. Just knock off one cat. Of course, it'll cost you 10 bucks to play. But I'll include a free practice shot."

The mark gave Shorty another twenty. "I'll take that practice shot, now." He stepped up to the counter and tossed the ball. It hit the cat perfectly and knocked it clear off the rack and into the net below. He announced, "O.K, I'm ready for the real thing." He tossed the ball again with what appeared to be the exact same shot into the cat's nose but with different results. A loser. And then another. The second twenty was now gone.

The mark's face puffed up in anger. He backed away from the counter, throwing up his hands. "That's enough," he cried. "I know you have to be controlling the game. I don't know how, but I know you are! I'd really like to know how you do it." He shook his head furiously. He was sure there was something fishy going on, but the exact explanation escaped him. He stomped off down the midway. Shorty disguised his glee.

I stayed behind, since this was now my chance to find out what the G really was. I looked Shorty in the eyes and asked, "So how'd you do it? I have to admit I'm baffled." Shorty grinned a gap-toothed smile and said, "When your Dad says its OK to tell you, that's when you'll know. Only when you're ready to turn out; you're too tender right now."

Shopping on the Road

Dad sat behind the wheel of the "shitbox," driving the two of us between spots. We were jumping from Provo, Utah in the north to St.George in the south part of the state. It was a long trip, but it took us through relaxing rustic scenery. We made a pit stop in the small town of Fillmore. Dad pulled into the parking lot of a small grocery. "Now I'm going to show you how to boost," he said. "Just watch me."

We entered the country store, a folksy wooden building with sawdust on the floor. An old man sat on a stool behind a cash register. "Help you, Mister?" he inquired innocently. Barry stood in front of him separated by a counter filled with sundries.

I watched Dad's hands as he engaged the clerk in a lengthy discussion about the weather. They were flying about in frequent gesticulations as he described a thunderstorm we had just weathered. I never saw him lift any merchandise. After about ten minutes, Dad purchased two cold soft drinks and we left. The transaction seemed completely normal.

When we got to the car I said, "I guess you changed your mind about boosting." Barry laughed and began to extract a myriad of items from his front jacket pocket: a pack of razor blades, a tube of toothpaste, a toothbrush, and three packages of chewing gum.

From his other pocket he withdrew a set of D-cell batteries, a jar of Vaseline and two packages of Twinkies. "Never pay for the small shit," he advised me. "You can save hundreds of dollars over the course of a year this way."

As we drove off, munching Twinkies and sipping soft drinks, he explained his rationale. "You see, we're the little guy, and our crimes are little. It's the big guys who are the real thieves," he insisted. "It's like this; the corporations who manufacture and sell everything we use get together and figure out ways to cheat the public like us. They have boards of directors who meet with the directors of other corporations to illegally fix prices."

Dad was on a roll. He continued, "Then they cheat on their taxes so that the average guy has to pay more than his fair share to the government. They use substandard equipment to save money and cheat their employees out of a decent wage. All in all, it's the guy in the street who gets screwed. The best way to get even is to steal. What we take is the only way we have of evening things out. It's not really stealing, son. It's just our way of balancing things out. Otherwise you just get screwed your whole life."

He seemed satisfied with this explanation and went on. "When the carnival comes into town, the motels raise their prices. Instead of paying the regular rate, carnies have to pay an extra premium. We have no choice. They got us by the balls. If we want to work, we have to pay outrageous prices. It's not right; it's just another way to steal from us. That's why we all roll out on restaurant tabs and steal the marks' money on the midway. It's just our way of equalizing things. They're as dirty as we are. Actually, come to think of it, we're superior—because we admit we're thieves. All those lying townspeople pretend they're honest. They can't admit the truth because it's not socially acceptable. They have to act like upstanding, churchgoing citizens. We accept who we are, at least. We make no pretense about who we are or what we do. We're actually far more honest."

I thought about his argument for a minute and asked, "How about the kids? They aren't trying to take anything from us." I continued, "or how about the hard-working farmers who are just trying to enjoy the county fair. Shouldn't we make exceptions for them?"

"Absolutely not," he retorted. "When the mooches come onto the midway and see the prizes available for a mere 25-cent investment, they get overtaken by their greed. They think they can get something for nothing. It appeals to the petty larceny in their hearts. Anyone who thinks about it for one minute has to realize that carnivals are not here to give away expensive toys for a quarter. But those cheap bastards don't think about that. They only think, 'Here's a chance to get something for nothing.' Bottom line is they're looking to steal something from us. An honest person would know better. So we're just taking advantage of people before they take advantage of us."

I considered this spin on his argument, then asked him,

"How about people who are just out for a good time? Or little kids who are too young to understand what's going on. They're not out to steal anything. Why should we trick them into losing their money?"

Dad took a long drag on his ever-present Chesterfield cigarette and answered, "There's nothing we do preventing people from having a good time though. They usually do anyway, even if they win nothing. So think of it this way: you're providing a public service. As for the little babies, they're going to lose their money no matter what. If you don't take it, the guy in the next joint will. Better to put bread on your own table than his."

A Christmas Gift

When I returned home for the fall semester, I entered Mount Vernon Junior High School, located near Washington Blvd. and Crenshaw Blvd. It was a lower class neighborhood than West Adams and had a large black enrollment. I had not yet had much exposure to black kids and some of them looked pretty scary. I was not a fighter and shied away from physical confrontations. When they did happen, I usually had to give up my lunch money.

I tried to hang out with the kids I knew from Cienega Elementary and make as few waves as possible. The whole experience was a bit overwhelming for me, and for the first time in my life my report card showed almost all "C"s. My parents, who never took notice of such things, went about their business, whatever that was.

The carnival was largely a summer affair. During the long off-season, carnies had to find other scams to get by. I was ignorant of just what my dad did to survive. I was busy with school and my afternoon newspaper job.

And Hebrew School. My parents, who had never been to a temple or synagogue in their lives, suddenly decided that I should be bar mitzvahed. There was no time to lose since I was quickly approaching the age of thirteen. Apparently there was no way I could "be a man" without going through the bar mitzvah ceremony. There was a Hebrew School a couple of miles from my house. My mom enrolled me and my brother, Ricki. Once or twice a week, we bicycled to classes after school. We learned nothing. I was taught to read and pronounce written Hebrew, but not what any of it meant.

Each week, it was total pandemonium. Every kid in the class was a mess-up whose parents dumped them off to get rid of them for a few hours. Most of them paid no attention to anything the old man with the yarmulke had to say, preferring instead to do arm-farts or engage in belching contests.

I was one of a couple of kids who made an earnest effort to master the language, even if I didn't know what it meant. It was an ancient language, and I thought maybe just reciting the words would reap some unknown benefit. It was like solving a puzzle. All those strange-looking letters could actually be pronounced. I got a certain charge out of learning to read aloud, rapidly. Mr. Kissel, our teacher, was thrilled to have ANYONE to teach.

The best part of my life was hanging out with a small cluster of friends at a tree house outside one of the guys' houses. Billy Lewand was my best friend. There was little Tommy, Ray and Jimmie and a couple of others who dropped in from time to time. We all had bicycles and pretty much permission to take off whenever we wanted to.

One time we went to a Boy Scout meeting but they wouldn't let us in, so we left the building and let the air out of the tires of all the bikes parked out in front.

Sometimes we rode our bikes up into the Baldwin Hills to tramp around. Occasionally, an older boy would bring a BB gun to shoot at jackrabbits. There were a great number of rabbits jumping here and there in the fields. We took a lot of shots but never actually hit one. I was secretly glad. I would have hated to see an injured bunny.

Mostly I played ball in my spare time. I played at school until the schoolyard was closed and then on the street in front of the house with the neighbor kids. Only when it became too dark to see the ball would we go into the house.

Although there was a steady stream of visitors who had secretive meetings with my folks, it didn't impact my life so I paid little attention. I was used to seeing shady characters on the carnival, so it just seemed normal.

What I didn't know was that Dad had been busted by L.A.P.D. undercover narcs for shooting up in a public restroom. He had been sentenced to serve six months in L.A. County Jail. He was due to surrender the first week of January, 1953.

Although I was enrolled in Hebrew School and well aware of the fact that I was Jewish, it had no impact on the way I viewed the world. Religion was not a part of my life or a part of the life of any of the kids I hung out with.

In the weeks leading up to Christmas, I sang Christmas carols in school, constructed crudely made Christmas cards for my family and looked forward to the Big Day as much as any other kid. My parents offered scant resistance to our demand for a Christmas tree.

It made perfect sense to me. Why should the Christians have all the good holidays? So our anticipation of the Great Day was as high in our house as any of our neighbors. Our parents fed us the Santa Claus story with a straight face. He would visit our home on Christmas Eve and leave a load of brightly colored packages. By the time the day actually arrived, we could hardly sleep.

Christmas Day, 1952. I was the first one awake in the still dark house. I stealthily made my way to the living room and discovered a treasure trove scattered under the tree. I noticed a strange smell as well. It smelled like natural gas. The odor was quite strong. I thought I had better notify my parents.

Even though there was a taboo concerning entering their bedroom, I felt that this situation warranted an exception. I pushed open the door and saw only Mom asleep. I called out and shook her slightly. She awoke, groggily and said, "What's happening?"

I said, "There's a gas smell in the house." She snapped to attention and sprung out of bed. I followed her into the living room where she flung open the door to the closet.

Inside, Dad was slumped against the wall. The gas jet near the bottom of the closet was turned on full blast. Barry's body fell towards the opening. Mom and I broke his fall by catching him just before he hit the floor. We laid him out gently on the carpet. Mom shut off the gas jet then rushed to the windows and threw them wide open. Then she returned to the prone body and said, "Help me get him up."

We each took one of his arms and flung it across our shoulders and began to walk/drag his body around the room. That's the way we spent the entire Christmas morning. After awhile he began to walk under his own power and mom brewed a pot of hot coffee while I continued to steady him.

Eventually he regained full consciousness and sat down at the kitchen table. Only then did the full impact of what had happened hit me. "My daddy just tried to KILL HIMSELF!" I thought. I felt weak and ill and retreated to my bed. The trauma was so intense that I felt a compulsion to bury the images in the darkest recesses of my being. For a brief moment, the furthest depth of my psyche opened up so that I could deposit this shocking event. I was surprised to see the other forgotten memory of the night at the Ocean Park house with the blood and the gun, alive and well just sitting there staring out at me.

It had been over three years, but the images were as bright and clear as if they had just happened. I had a perfectly preserved tape of the entire event including detailed pictures and the overwhelming feeling of horror.

I wanted to stuff this shocking brush with suicide into the black vault of obliterated memory as quickly as possible and seal the door shut.

I was amazed to find those old horror shots alive and well preserved. Now I had a new tape to hide away. I had to do it fast before any more unwanted recollections intruded on my consciousness. I had seen enough. I mustn't EVER open that box again.

And then the old man was gone. Off to jail. So I assumed the mantle of "Man of the House" a little over a year before my bar-mitzvah would formally certify me as such. It wasn't that big of a deal since dad was on the road at least half the year anyway. I was not told where he was or what he was doing. More importantly, I was not told how we were supposed to survive without an income.

As it turned out, not paying the rent on the house we were living in was part of the solution. The owner of our house was on an extended business trip in the Philippines and had left the collecting of the rent to the bank. The bank dutifully sent out overdue notices every month. They were just as dutifully deposited in the trash. It went on like that for months.

For my part everything seemed just fine. Baseball, work, Hebrew School, bicycles and tree houses. Life was good.

Life Without Papa

In many ways, our life was much more settled with Dad behind bars. There were fewer visitors to the house. It was sort of an Ozzie and Harriet life, only with Ozzie in jail. Children played in the street day and night. Kids ran into and out of everybody else's house, and raided refrigerators as well. Unlocked bikes were carelessly dumped onto sidewalks and lawns. There was a new thing called television. It was like radio, but with pictures like a movie theatre.

The first family on our block to have a television set lived almost directly across the street from us. The family had two kids, Alan and Billy. They immediately became my best friends. A gang of us invaded their living room to watch *Beanie and Cecil the Seasick Sea Serpent* after school each day. Their mom gave us lemonade and oatmeal cookies. Afternoons at their house became a neighborhood ritual.

There was one piece of unexpected news. Mom was pregnant. After eight years of believing that child-bearing was a thing of the past for her, she found herself with child once again. I thought it was a burdensome new responsibility, but no one consulted me. I was not altogether certain how babies were made, so I withheld any comment.

Junior high life became infinitely better when I began to hang out with Loren Schweninger, the best athlete in our class. He was also the best fighter, which made life much easier for me. No one wanted to mess with me when he was nearby, which I made sure was nearly always. Loren lived with his mother, Wanda, and little brother Mark.

His mom was a soft-spoken woman who commanded the respect of her two sons with apparently no effort whatever. She exuded an aura of kindness and charity which never changed no matter how many times I saw her. I was amazed that a family could operate on such a cooperative level.

We played tackle football without pads at Rancho Park next to Dorsey High School on weekends. It was a bit nuts, but we suffered no serious injuries. No one could actually bring Loren down alone, but I gave it my all. I discovered that I actually liked hitting and getting hit. For someone who had tried to avoid any kind of fist fight, I discovered a competitive urge that allowed me to mix it up on the football field. What I lacked in physical skills I made up for with determination and effort. I was an asset to the team by spirit alone.

Loren, on the other hand, was just head and shoulders above everyone else. He had real ability. So much so, in fact, that he went on to acquire a scholarship to play football at the University of Colorado at Boulder where he became a standout linebacker and fullback. He starred in the Orange Bowl when the Buffaloes faced the LSU Tigers. Loren intercepted a pass early in the game and ran it in for a touchdown, giving Colorado what turned out to be their only lead of the game.

One spring afternoon, while Dad was away, my mom took me to Woolworth's to seek a refund for a purchase she wanted to return. We entered the store and she immediately went to the nearest cashier. "I'd like to return this item," she stated.

The lady at the register replied, "I'll be happy to exchange it for you." Mom shook her head and said, "I don't want to exchange it. I want my money back."

The cashier informed her that the store did not give cash refunds, but it might be possible to get a credit slip. Mom bristled, "I paid cash and I want cash back, not an exchange and not a credit slip." She crossed her arms in front of her, defiantly. The lady at the register repeated, "We do NOT make cash refunds here. I already told you that."

"And I told you that I paid cash and that's exactly what I want back," Mom insisted. Several customers were lined up waiting to pay for their goods. They listened intently to the exchange between Mom and the clerk, wondering who would prevail.

The cashier was becoming flustered and called for the store manager. A short guy with a thin moustache and slight paunch soon appeared and inquired, "What seems to be the problem here?" Mom spat out, "This idiot refuses to return my money."

The manager smiled and said solicitously, "We have a store policy which prevents us from giving cash refunds."

Mom shot back, "I'm not interested in your store policy. I just want my money back—*NOW!*" The heated exchange attracted a crowd which began to press closer for a better look.

The manager suggested, "I'm sure we can resolve this matter amicably. Please follow me to my office." Mom, who was beginning to flush bright red retorted, "I'm not going *anywhere* with you. We're going to settle this right here. Now am I going to get my money back or not?"

The manager replied, "Please, ma'am, there is no need to raise your voice." Mom's anger was reaching hysterical heights. "Yes there IS A NEED TO RAISE MY VOICE. You jerks are in the wrong and you know it. Give me my money back now!"

I began to wish that I were somewhere else. It was obvious that the store had a fixed policy and Mom had no chance of getting what she wanted. This was a project doomed to failure. But there was no convenient escape route available and Mom had me firmly by the hand, anyway.

The store manager protested, "I'm sorry, it's not my decision. There is a corporate policy that covers all of our stores. It absolutely forbids any cash refunds." Mom replied, "I don't give a damn about your store policy. You can't take people's money and then decide to not return it. I'm not going to stand for it." Then she screamed at the top of her lungs, "And I'm not leaving until I have that money in my hand. Do you understand?"

I was beginning to wish an earthquake would hit the store, split open the floor and swallow me.

The manager looked up at the growing crowd, attracted by the fireworks, and then made a decision, "Give her the money," he directed the cashier, then turned about and headed back to his office. The lady at the check-out counter sneered, then reluctantly drew a few bills from the register and held them out to Mom, who promptly snatched them and whirled towards the door, dragging me with her.

"*Assholes!*" Mom exclaimed as we hit the street. "Don't you ever let them take advantage of you. And don't take 'No' for an answer. When you know you're right, you HAVE to stand up and be heard."

I saw my mother in a whole new light. She had a reserve

of inner strength I had never suspected. Through sheer force of character, she had forced a national corporation with countless outlets throughout the U.S. to change their store policy. It was unimaginable. My young brain was reeling. She had taught me a lesson I was never to forget. It was all about the force of one person who refuses to buckle under to an invisible power structure. I would have the courage of my convictions for as long as I lived.

Homecoming

Barry was released from jail when Mom was about five months pregnant. He had missed nearly the entire carnival season and was therefore broke. He was on probation and had to work at a regular job. For the first time in his life, my dad was required to do an honest day's labor. He got a job with a moving company. He got up in the morning and went to work. It was a novel experience for him. He made enough money to pay for groceries and utilities, but not rent.

He became depressed and turned once again to heroin to ease the pain. He connected at the Grand Central Market downtown, where there was apparently more on sale than just fruits and vegetables. He brought the smack home and cut it enough so that he could sell some and pay for his own habit.

After a short time, Mom joined him in shooting up. Soon they were both engulfed in a drugged-out state of being. My brother and I were blissfully unaware of their addiction and lived life as though everything were perfectly normal.

At the beginning of 1954, I had a surprise waiting for me when I got home from school. Mom was gone. She had been taken off to L.A. County Hospital to cope with a baby that had arrived two months early.

The doctors at the hospital were baffled as to why she was giving birth prematurely. In those days, there was little information on the effects of heroin on pregnancy. No one guessed that the baby was fully addicted at birth. And Mom didn't tell them.

The baby weighed in at just over three pounds and was placed into an incubator. Her life was hanging by a thread while she struggled both to survive and overcome heroin withdrawal symptoms at the same time. For several weeks, it was touch and go. Faye knew the baby's life hung in the balance, but she couldn't bring herself to tell the doctors the truth. It probably would have meant a trip to jail for both her and Barry, and neither of them was willing to take that chance, even if the baby died.

It was a miracle that my little sister made it. Three weeks

after her birth, she was cleared to be released from the hospital. It was not a great homecoming. The dark cloud that had been hanging over the house was about to become a full-blown storm. Our landlord, Mr. Wells, returned from Manila only to discover that his tenants had made no rental payments for the past year. He wanted revenge.

I had no warning when that fateful day with the moving van arrived. It was a Saturday morning and I was planning to take my bike to the park to play baseball. But there was no time for baseball since my entire world was about to come crashing about me. Life would never be the same again.

PART II

The Gardens

I never started out to be a *vato* from the East L.A. barrio, *ese*. I didn't know what a *vato* was. I didn't know what the *barrio* was. I didn't know what *ese* meant.

But I soon learned. There was a whole Mexican culture thriving in the projects. For these newcomers to America, the projects looked pretty good. Running water and indoor plumbing were a big advantage. Sometimes it helped for me to see my surroundings through their eyes. It could have been worse.

We eventually cleared our apartment of roaches, although a few of the old-timers insisted on retiring there and we didn't have the heart to evict them. Rich people don't know what it's like to have to fight roaches. It's a full-time battle. Living in Ramona Gardens meant living with roaches. It was a given.

Located a couple miles east of the L.A. County General Hospital, you get there off of Soto Street at Marengo. Soto Street passes alongside a verdant park with tall trees. At Lancaster Street, you turn right towards the hill that will drop you into the lowlands leading into the projects.

A series of low-slung military-type beige bungalows provided housing for two thousand families, virtually all of whom were black or Mexican. Living in the projects was just one step removed from living in the street. It was the lowest rung of the ladder. There were no restaurants, movie theaters, or any commercial enterprises whatever, except for one grocery, Abe's Market. It was an insular community with rigid, unwritten laws. Just outside the projects was a neighborhood of broken down houses with weed-strewn yards. We could only dream of living in that kind of luxury.

The black gangs gathered on one side of Lancaster Street across from the market. The Mexican gangs converged on the opposite corner. It made a trip to the market a challenging experience. The first time I was sent to pick up groceries, the black guys forcibly took my money. The next time, I tried skirting along the other side of the street. Then the Mexicans took my groceries after leaving the store. I realized that I had to find a new route or we would starve.

I scouted the neighborhood for alternate routes and discovered a back way to get to Abe's. It was twice as far, but I found that I could get in and out without being held up. Finding alternate routes around the gangs became my primary job. It was like a game. I would dash from bush to bush, crouching to see if the road was clear.

I had similar problems getting to school and then back home. Lincoln High School was two miles from our home. The passage led through Lincoln Park, basically gang central. I was stopped and unburdened of my pocket money several times before I found a circuitous course that allowed me relative safety.

I was relieved though to discover that gangsters demanded only money. I was convinced that my very existence was at stake every time I left the house. I felt like a rabbit in a jungle filled with predators. Every waking moment was dedicated to plotting alternate escape plans. I developed a keen sense of early-warning signals and managed to avoid the most life-threatening confrontations.

My brother was not so lucky. He was still in grammar school and there was only one way to get to his building. He got trapped nearly every day and had to fight for his life. The school called and reported that he was attacked by several kids on the school grounds on a regular basis. But they offered no solutions. Ricki suffered greatly until he graduated and was able to attend school with me. Lincoln was both a junior high and high school combined in those years.

My first close call with serious injury came as I was exploring the neighborhood for safe trails going from school back to my house. It was twilight and I was passing through an unfamiliar part of the Gardens. I was walking down a concrete path when I spotted a group of about 20 guys surrounding a teenager who they had backed up against a wall. My first thought was to turn and run in the opposite direction. But they seemed so preoccupied with their current victim that I thought I could slip by without being noticed. I was wrong.

I tried to become invisible and pressed against the wall furthest from where the action was centered. I was almost in the clear when one of the guys on the perimeter spotted me. He left the cluster of guys and approached me. I froze in my tracks.

"You're in the wrong place, *ese*. Some things here you ain't supposed to see." He motioned towards the cluster of guys. I could see that the guy they had pinned against the wall was bleeding from a cut on his cheek. A guy in front of him was brandishing a knife. I diverted my gaze, wondering how I was going to avoid a similar fate.

Darkness was settling in and I was getting more nervous by the second. The *cholo* in front of me leaned in towards my face. I was waiting for some cold steel to drag across my cheek when suddenly he said, "Ain't you the new kid at Lincoln? I seen you in the cafeteria." I nodded without saying a word. He glared at me so closely I could see the gold tooth in the back of his mouth. "Get the fuck outta here, *ese*," he threatened. "And don't never come back."

I didn't need a second invitation. I moved as stealthily as I could past the throng with their backs to me. It worked and I was able to make it home safely. I took his advice and never returned.

The overall effect of living in the gang-dominated neighborhood weighed on me like a medieval suit of armor. In fact, I wished I could wear thick metal coveralls. Without any defenses, I was more than willing to go through life like the Tin Man in the Wizard of Oz.

I learned to develop a mental attitude similar to a hunted animal. I devised an approach to life that combined camouflage, stealth, and a keen sense of survival. The enemy was everywhere. There was no real escape, only temporary respites. I plotted each of my outings with the military planning of General Patton. Every trip to the bus, school or the market required a well thought-out blueprint followed by keen execution. I had to devise and craft the proper approach to each goal. A single slip-up could spell disaster.

I began figuring out alternative routes well in advance of everywhere I had to go. I had back-up plans for everything. I wore dark clothing at night, and skulked about in the shadows. I went to school hours before classes began. I had to foresee every possible situation before it occurred. I was like a spy in the enemy camp. Capture was a fate too scary to consider. There was no room for error. I couldn't count on luck.

Homelife

Within a matter of a few weeks, our apartment was transformed into a "Shooting Gallery" for the neighborhood junkies. I was introduced to the new crowd that made 1342 Crusado Lane their second home. Dad had made friends with some of the locals quickly. And they, just as quickly, made themselves comfortable in our house.

Often I opened the front door and was greeted by Carlitos, our neighbor from three doors down, who came in and nodded out on our couch where he lapsed into the semi-conscious state that follows the "Rush" an injection of heroin brings on. He got lost in some morphine dream world.

The "Rush" was what it was all about. The immediate cessation of all pain, all worries, and all problems. The drug offered relief from the difficulties of life. Its seduction appealed to those looking for an easy way out. With a single shot, all of life's imperfections are instantly replaced by an incomparable high. It is both immediate and powerful. A moment of extreme ecstasy. There is no time or space. The hopelessness of being trapped in the projects is replaced by castles in the sky, a kingdom of pure bliss. Grinding poverty transformed into untold wealth. The enormous struggle of everyday life at the bottom is replaced by a jolly frolic with the gods. It is a mighty temptation for a weak, stressed-out soul.

The side effects were, however, disastrous both to the user and his family. The drug demanded constant attention. If you weren't using IT, you were out looking for IT or you were out stealing to get IT. Very quickly, every waking thought and action is driven by IT. The be all and end all—*IT!*

Across the living room from Carlitos was the sprawled out body of Horseface Joe. His legs dangled over one arm of the old overstuffed chair. Horseface had long arms, one of which nearly touched the ground. The other covered his eyes. When I entered the room, he roused himself slightly, "Oh, Kenny. How you doin' man? You got books?" he asked thickly through his droopy moustache. "Thas' good, man. Stay in school." Then he drifted back into his private world, his heavy-lidded eyes slowly closing.

I went straight upstairs to my room. At the top of the stairs, as I passed the bathroom, the door opened and out came Barry and another slightly built white guy named Leo, who was my dad's running partner. The bathroom was full of smoke and emitted a peculiar acrid odor. We nodded briefly to each other as we passed. I grunted, "Hi Leo. Hi Dad."

I was living life in a bubble. I managed to become oblivious to everything going on around me, except school and my books. I somehow knew that education was my only way out of this mess. I went to school early and stayed late. I volunteered for extra-curricular activities. I went out for sports teams. Anything to keep me in school. And away from my house.

School was my island of sanity. No doped-up junkies, no graffiti, no gangs. A pretty campus with lots of trees and green lawns— and teachers who really knew their stuff. I had found a home. I loved Abraham Lincoln High School.

I wasn't sure they loved me though. In fact, I'm sure they didn't. I was among a small minority of white kids at school and the only Jew. And worse, I was one of the bottom 10% living in the projects. I didn't fit in anywhere. I must have come off as remote and distant or superior to the punks surrounding me. Getting good grades in that school did not help my popularity. It made me seem to be a kiss-ass.

So there I was, with no friends, heroin junkies for parents, a shooting-gallery for a home, and living in constant fear of the gangs. Welcome to puberty.

The Delgados, A.J. and Melvin

Directly across the lane from us lived the Delgados. I didn't know it at the time, but they were to be my saviors. Mama Delgado lived with her five children in a unit identical to ours. Fortunately for me, all five were good-looking girls. The eldest was Lupe, who was the first to leave the house. She was also the first to return, bringing with her two small infants she had acquired during her brief journey outside the family home. Now there were three generations of Delgados living in the three-bedroom apartment.

The other girls were teenagers, ranging from Rosie, a full-blooded beauty, to Dolores, also gorgeous and next in line, to Mary, who was to be my close confidant throughout my years in the projects, to Bertha a budding eleven-year old.

They were to become my second family. In a manner of speaking, they were more important than my first family. I could always walk out my front door and twenty paces away, enter theirs. Their openness and acceptance of me was total and complete. There was never any question as to why I was a constant presence in their home. It was just OK.

I had never seen Mexican culture up close. It amazed me how full and complete it was. Even in the midst of grinding poverty, there was laughter, warmth, and a spirit of life. And food. Tamale feasts prepared to feed a hungry army. Fiestas seemed to come up with amazing regularity and the Delgado's home was party central.

I don't know how they managed it, but there was always more than enough to go around. Nobody ever left the Delgados hungry. No matter how large the crowd of family and friends, there was a feeling of plenty and giving.

I'm not sure why they accepted me so completely, but I wasn't asking any questions. I'm pretty sure they knew my own home was a disaster. To their credit they never brought up the subject of all the low-life scum coming and going at all hours at my place. For that I will be eternally grateful.

With so many beautiful daughters, there were lots and lots of visitors at their place too. You never knew who you would find in their living room when you entered. But the vibes were always good.

I never had real sex with any of the girls, but there was a great deal of fooling around. I reveled in being surrounded by so many delectable teenagers. The other guys in the neighborhood and at school were green with envy. They had scoped out those girls closely and couldn't figure out how to get close to them. I, on the other hand, had total access whenever I chose. Outside of school, the Delgados were the most important part of my life.

The friendship they offered me meant far more than anyone might have guessed. Even the craziness in their mostly unkempt house, created by so many people living in such close quarters, seemed like an island of sanity to me. Compared to the activities going on in my house, their place was an ivory tower.

The closest I came to any type of romance with any of the Delgado girls was with Mary. Although we never became boyfriend and girlfriend, we played around a lot. It seemed natural because we spent so much time together. She was easy to talk to and a year or two younger than I. Mary was short with curly, black hair.

Although not a raving beauty, she had a warmth and cuteness that made her an ideal friend. I could open up and discuss anything with her, except, of course, what was going on in my house just twenty yards away. She and I practiced the latest dance steps and she taught me the cha-cha, the hottest dance craze in the Latino community. Thanks to her, I became a passable dancer.

I was fortunate enough to make friends with two exceptional black guys, A.J. and Melvin, both of whom lived in the projects and also attended Lincoln. A.J., whose real name was Henry Bernard (I never did find out where the "A.J." came from) was a slender, casual guy with an easygoing demeanor. He had a ready smile and was totally accepting of me. He was also the best all-around athlete I had ever known. There was no sport at which he did not effortlessly excel. In another day and age he would have been highly recruited by a number of colleges.

As it was, he wore his grace and agility as though it were no big deal. He was a friend I could walk to school with and whose attitude made life easier for me. Although he never knew it, A.J. was my hero. He glided through the projects with a princely bearing that belied his family's meager living circumstances. To the casual observer, he might have appeared to be a gifted boy who treated life as though it were a simple affair, requiring no effort whatever. It seemed to me that his feet barely touched the ground whenever we walked to or from school. I felt like a plough horse next to a thoroughbred.

Melvin was a different kind of cat. About the same height as A.J., Melvin was the owner of a fabulously sculpted body which he used to great advantage on the school gymnastics team. He could hold an iron cross on the rings steady, without the hint of a shake or shiver longer than anyone ought to humanly be able to do it. He was definitely the standout of the team. His attitude was considerably different than the outgoing A.J. He walked with a stoic glide and spoke little. His physical presence was enough of a message to local tough guys stating in no uncertain terms, "Don't mess with me." And no one did. I admired Melvin immensely, and was grateful for his friendship even though we never related with the ease and depth I had with A.J.

Melvin and A.J. were the first black friends I ever had. There were plenty of other blacks in the projects but those two guys exuded a type of class that was exceptional. It was as though they had found some secret allowing them to rise above the miserable surroundings in which they found themselves.

They were role models for me, although I'm sure they were never aware of it. I was grateful that they accepted me without reservation. They invited me to parties where I was the only white kid present. It was a little strange at first, but the black teenagers only wanted to dance and have a good time just like the parties at the Delgados. My race was never an issue. Although the blacks and Mexicans kept separate from each other, neither seemingly had a problem with my presence. In time, I could move effortlessly from one group to the other.

Inside my home, minorities were referred to as Spics and Spades. I rankled at this type of language largely because so

96

many of our economically deprived neighbors seemed morally superior to my own parents. The irony of the situation was lost on Mom and Dad, who used racial slurs to try to elevate themselves above the crowd populating the projects.

Blacks were also referred to as "Jigs" and Mexicans "Greasers." I hated the racial epithets and wrote it off as the last, desperate gasp of the ignorant white, prejudiced generation from which they had come.

These slurs were also common jargon on the carnival lot. Carnies used Pig-Latin or what they called "Ee-iz" slang to cover their put-down words. A brief summary of the "Ee-iz" language goes as follows: Any word can be disguised by adding these two syllables in the middle of the pronunciation of it. For example, the word "Mark" becomes "Mee-iz-ark." The word "Show" becomes "Shee-iz-ow." The word "Blow" becomes "Blee-iz-ow."

After a little practice and hearing the slang used over and over, you can get quite adept at disguising anything you don't want the public to understand. As an insider language, it permitted the carnies to communicate with each other without having to whisper into another's ear or give visual hand signs that could be spotted.

Montana 1953

Ekalaka, Montana—the end of the line. Remotest part of the southeast section of the state. Spittin' distance to North Dakota. Carter County Fair was a big deal in these parts, and with Ekalaka being the county seat, it was the proud possessor of the county's fairgrounds.

The season was running down for me. Dad and I had escaped the steamy L.A. summer, leaving the rest of the family to deal with the housing project on their own. We had spent the entire summer crisscrossing this enormous state, moving week to week from one celebration to another. It was nearly time for me to go back to school.

That summer I saw more livestock shows, jam and jelly contests, and 4-H exhibits than any living human. I spent my spare time hanging out in horse barns and championship produce displays where I learned a lot about agriculture and farming, and what real apple pie tastes like. And also how cute farm girls are.

Having been with the same show all season, I had my run of the midway. I knew all the carnies, the gypsies and the ride boys. I was a regular in the "grab joints," which fried up burgers for the carnies. The "grab joints" were the social center of the carnival. If you were on a break and didn't feel like leaving the lot, there was always someone to hang with and talk to.

Most carny talk centered around who scored big and who had to kick back a big score. They called it "cuttin up touches." Everyone had stories.

Balloonhead Bill had stories about loose women on the midway. Blackie Stein had touches about Native Americans, meaning he had countless stories of playing Indian reservations in his earlier days. Thousand Face Foxy, so named in honor of his countless facial twitches, nailed a mark for a thousand dollars at the state fair in Texas in twenty minutes.

But you never knew how much of what you heard to believe. Clearly there were many colorful rip-offs, but just as clearly there was much fiction. Either way it was entertaining. For the most part, carnies had only a passing acquaintanceship with the truth. It was not a virtue to be pursued.

Certainly stealing from each other was a common occurrence. Every carny was hip to the H.O., holding out on the boss. Bosses knew that the agents were not turning in all the money. They had been agents themselves. So internal stealing was permitted as long as it wasn't too blatant. It was in everyone's interest not to notice. In fact, the subject NEVER came up. It was taboo. Everyone knew everyone else was a dyed-in-the-wool thief, but it was forbidden to talk about stealing from each other. Even Dad, who had a philosophical justification for every other type of thievery, had nothing to say on the subject of short-changing other carnies. Therefore nothing was said.

The bosses hoped that their agents would not steal too much. If they held out too much, you'd have to replace them. But if you were a really good agent, then you could steal more because they wanted to keep you. They would rather hire a good agent who steals a lot than a bad one who doesn't steal as much. It's a delicate balancing act. The perennial question was: Is it better to have a hotshot who's going to steal you blind but still manages to turn in a large take, or hire some dumbo who turns in less money because he's lame?

I accepted the life of a thief and Dad's rationalizations as to why it was not really immoral. It's amazing that I was able to adjust so easily. Before going on the road with him, I had had honest jobs like selling newspapers or mowing lawns. It never occurred to me to steal. But with Dad, I developed into an accomplished thief on the carnival lot, never missing a beat.

I have to admit that I enjoyed life on the road. I got to stay up late, sleep in, hang out with the carnies and make good money, tax free. I later discovered that no one paid income tax, ever. As Barry explained, "Don't get a social security card and don't file taxes. If you NEVER file, they don't know you exist." He had gone a lifetime living below the IRS radar.

Shorty

Shorty Karns was the slickest six-cat operator of all time. He had been in the carnival business so long that some said he invented the six-cat. He was so small that he had to stand on a wooden box just to see over the top of the counter. He wore a plaid vest and matching hat with an ever-present monstrous black cigar clenched in his teeth. He had been offering alibis to marks for so long, he invented an entirely new set of excuses to cool out marks. "Perhaps you would do better standing on one leg," he suggested helpfully to one player. To another, "Try resting your off hand on your head." One time I saw him convince a mark to "hold your left nut," while firing the ball.

I hung out around Shorty's joint so often he finally turned me on to the "G" or "Gaff" attached to the game. It was so startlingly simple that I was amazed that I had been unable to guess it on my own. It all centered on the canvas net which held the balls used in the game. The net hung loosely from a board which stretched across the underside of the counter on the agent's side. To the untrained eye, there was nothing suspicious or unusual about the setup. It appeared to just be a convenient way to hold spare balls.

I was amazed when Shorty showed me how it worked. When the agent leaned against the board holding the balls, it activated a wooden shelf located under the cats. The shelf could be removed as a barrier by the operator's movement of his knee against the board. If he wanted to show a mark how easy it was to knock a cat off the shelf and into the net below, he would casually lean forward to release the shelf and the cat would fall unimpeded into the net below. If he did not lean against the board, the shelf remained in place and prevented any cat from falling all the way off. It was foolproof.

One day in Ekalaka, a mean, nasty Montana cowboy was going up against the six-cat. I was used to seeing rough guys on the lot, but this one was different. He looked as tough as the spare ribs at a Polish butcher shop. And he had money. Shorty's eyes became as large as saucers when he got a gander at the mark's poke. The cowboy's wallet bulged with $20 bills. The carny's tired old heart sprang to life as he realized that this could be his score of the year. A true jackpot. Gold at the end of the carny rainbow. Nirvana!

Shorty bristled with a spirit that belied his 78 years. I was deeply moved by his honest, childlike greed. He was running his standard line hot and heavy, and the cowboy was sucking it up. His suntanned face wore a determined expression. His eyes remained steady and fixed on the target. He was intent on winning this game. He appeared to be a person who was not used to losing at anything. Shorty was just barely able to conceal his glee in the presence of such commitment. And all those bills in the fat wallet.

Shorty had run the old "jackpot in the cigar box" scam on the mark. As long as the sucker played the game, all his money went into the box and would be given back to him when he won. The idea was to sell the concept that he couldn't lose as long as he could afford to keep playing. The catch was that he had to pay the total amount in the box for each shot.

The game escalated from $5 per throw to $10 and then to $20. Each shot brought the promise of winning the contents of the cigar box plus any three prizes in the joint. And each shot also brought the disappointment of losing another wad of money. I could see frustration building in the eyes of the cowboy. I wondered if Shorty saw it as well.

The mark had mastered the art of tossing the ball and hitting the cat perfectly on its red nose. But on the money shot, it stubbornly refused to fall all the way off the shelf. Shorty alibied that the shot was a little low, although I noticed he wasn't even looking. I was sure that the mark must have noticed also, but he continued to play on. He peeled off $40, then $80, and then $160, losing each time.

The player's frustration began to show. His aim became shaky and he began to waver, clearly missing his target. This, of course, gave credence to Shorty's alibis. The lanky Montana cowboy stopped for a moment, stood tall, stretched and paced in front of the six-cat, trying to regain control. Shorty helpfully offered him a free practice throw which resulted in a perfect shot, one that Shorty allowed to fall off the shelf. "Now just match the pot, do that same shot again and you have a big winner," he exclaimed.

The cowboy counted out $320, took the ball and studied it. His throw caught the cat right between the eyes at just the right speed. Shorty was into an alibi even before the cat got hung up on the shelf.

The young man glared at Shorty and said, "I say I hit it perfectly." The carny retorted that it was impossible or the cat would have fallen all the way off the shelf.

The mark simply reached into his back pocket and produced more money. There was a thick wad of $100 bills. If Shorty had been younger, he would have climaxed on the spot. The player handed over $640 without so much as batting an eyelash. He missed. Then he missed again for $1,280. When he began to count out $2,500, I noticed Shorty begin to lose some of his enthusiasm. He was not emotionally equipped to deal with that much money. He began to wish that the determined young man would give up and go home. But the set of the mark's jaw spoke otherwise. He would not quit. Shorty ceased to encourage the mark to play on.

But his greed overcame his sense of impending danger as he scooped up the $2,500 and deposited it into the cigar box. Another loser. Without a word, the mark began to count out the money for the next game. Shorty was now genuinely shaken. He gently suggested, "Maybe today is just not your day."

The cowboy stopped counting and, for the first time, allowed his emotions to show. "You tellin' me to quit?" he asked with a quiet threat in his voice. "No sir," Shorty replied timidly. "Just trying to help."

The player tilted back his western hat and glared into Shorty's eyes. "There's nothing phony about this game, is there?" he challenged.

"No sir," replied Shorty weakly.

The saddle-hardened young man began to count out hundred dollar bills. He stopped when he realized that he was $1,300 short of the amount needed to match the pot. The fact that ALL of his money was gone seemed to come as a complete surprise to him. He was obviously not used to being out of money. When the full impact of the situation hit him, he lashed out and grabbed Shorty by his vest, pulling him halfway over the counter.

"This whole setup is a fake, isn't it?" he said accusingly. Shorty's collar was now choking him so tightly he could barely breathe. His short legs were flailing helplessly in the air. The cowboy relaxed his grip on the shaken carny and regained his composure. He said evenly, "I'm going to the parking lot to get the rest of my money from my car. I'm going to take one last shot at that cat, and believe me I'm going to win." The way he said it made me believe that he WOULD win even though I knew Shorty controlled the outcome.

When he departed, Shorty let out a sigh of relief. He stated to me that he hoped the mark would not return once he had a chance to realize that there was no sense in throwing good money after bad. His equilibrium restored, he began to regale me with stories of other lucrative scores he had made. He was in the middle of one of his stories when he spied the cowboy striding purposefully down the midway towards the joint. There was nowhere to hide. The mark had seen him.

When he approached, I could see that he had returned to his quiet, determined demeanor. He pulled his billfold from his rear pocket and began to deliberately count out fifty $100 bills. He handed them to Shorty who quietly deposited them into the cigar box and handed him a ball.

The young man studied the ball a moment, then reached into his waistband and produced a .45 caliber handgun. He then reached into his pants pocket and extracted a bullet which he carefully loaded into the pistol. He picked up the gun and aimed it at Shorty.

Shorty started to speak when the mark interrupted him saying, "Don't say a word. I'm not going to shoot you. Not yet. First I'm going to hit that cat with this ball and it is going to fall off the shelf." He placed the loaded gun on the counter and added, "This gun says it's going to fall off."

I retreated to the far corner of the joint, not really wanting to see what happened next, but unable to avert my eyes.

The cowboy pitched the ball and hit the cat squarely on the nose at just the right speed. The cat tumbled backwards but came to rest still on the shelf. A loser.

The man reached for his gun, aimed it at Shorty's head, held it a moment, then said, "If that cat had fallen off the shelf, I would have known that this game was rigged." He then inserted the gun back into his waistband, turned and stalked off.

Shorty was ashen. I ran to him as it looked like he might pass out. "Why did you do it, Shorty? Why did you catch the cat? He might have killed you," I exclaimed.

"I couldn't stand to lose all that money," he answered with a sigh.

The Flat Store

I spent many hours on the carnival lot watching my father work. His joint looked different from all the others on the midway. The tent itself was of a much higher quality than the others. It was ornately decorated with expensive prizes, tastefully displayed on purple crushed velvet covered shelves. It had the look of an upscale merchandise display, complete with gold watches, shiny new hunting rifles, and expensive household items. None of the other games looked remotely like the "flat store," the undisputed king of all carnival scams.

The agents who had mastered the joint were known as 'flatties.' They dressed and looked different than other carnies. The guys wore sharply pressed slacks, open necked sport shirts and well-made sports jackets. There were no female flatties. It was strictly a men's club.

The guys hung out all day by the pool of the best motel in town, or gambling and drinking in one of the well-appointed show trailers reserved for them. They slept late and showed up to work only after the sun went down. It was a privileged position that excused them from long hours on the midway and from ever doing any physical labor. They also earned more money than anyone except the show owners, who collected a steady income from ride receipts and weekly rental fees from each joint on the midway.

The flatties felt entitled to special treatment because of the years of training required to learn the intricacies of the flat store. They exuded an air of superiority when they made their nightly forays onto the midway. On the carnival lot, they looked pretty high-class, but in truth, they resembled used car salesmen.

The flat stores were so inherently evil that they required special permission from local law-enforcement to even set up on the fairgrounds. Each show had a designated "Patch Man" whose only job was to bribe local officials. He arrived in town a week before the rest of the show and held private meetings where he negotiated how many joints would be allowed, how much they could take from each mark and how profits would be distributed between the carnies and the Sheriff.

The Patch Man was indispensable because the flat stores generated a large number of complaints which were inevitably brought to the local police station. If the top cops were properly compensated, they would deflect the grievances with straight-faced warnings to aggrieved citizens about playing "games-of-chance."

Occasionally, the complaint would come from a well-connected local businessman and the cops would dutifully shut down the games and cart the carnies off to jail. That was a rare exception, and the agents were quietly released the next morning. The boys in blue had no desire to kill the goose laying their golden eggs. The nightly payoffs were in cash and far exceeded their normal pay. Each annual county fair could be counted on to provide a healthy bonus.

The games were generally of two types, either a "Count Store" or a "Peek Store." The Count Store relied on a wooden board 24- inches square with four-inch wooden slats on three sides, also known as a "Razz" board. The bottom board was covered with marble-sized indentations, each one of which had a number from one to six inscribed on it. The sucker was given a cup containing eight marbles and told to empty them onto the Razz board. The carny then added up the total of all eight marbles and referred the mark to a chart which contained every possible number combination. Each number on the chart had a value assigned to it ranging from zero points to 10 points. Ten points was a winner entitling the player to select from any prize in the house.

The Peek Store worked in a similar fashion. Instead of using marbles to get a number, the mark was told to toss a three-inch round rubber ring at the pins. There were three rows of clothespins stretched across the joint. The mark would select a pin by tossing one of the rubberized rings at the pins and thus hook one. Each pin had a number inscribed on the back which the carny then showed to the mark. He was then referred to the corresponding number on a chart. It was the same chart used by the count store. Once again 10 points was a winner.

What made the games so appealing was the prominent

display of so many obviously expensive prizes. The eye-appeal of the joint was its strong suit. There was seldom a crowd of players surrounding the counter. Flatties played to one mark at a time and each play could last a considerable time, from 20 minutes to a couple of hours. It was not a volume business.

For that reason the flat store agents were quite particular about who they called in to play the game. Not just ANY carnival-goer would do. The highly experienced carnies had a well-developed knack for knowing just who to select. It had to be someone with a substantial amount of money in his pocket. I say HIS pocket because they never played to women, nor to minors or old people. And seldom to minorities. The perfect mark was a white, dull-witted male with a fat wallet. Because each game involved a considerable investment of time, it was important to select the right goose. A good flattie could spot a ripe mark 50 yards away. It was a talent all its own, developed over years of practice. I studied the action every chance I got.

One evening in Miles City, Montana, I was hanging out by the Count Store talking to my Dad. He was showing me how to operate the Razz board. With his slicked back hair and pencil thin moustache, he resembled Snidley Whiplash or Oilcan Harry. I was constantly amazed that he could get people to trust him. He had this sickeningly saccharine personality that he had developed over the years, but it seemed to work well on a carnival lot.

"Dump the cup of marbles onto the board," he instructed. I did. The marbles scattered around the board, each one settling into a numbered indentation. "Now what total would you like to reach?" he asked. I looked at him questioningly. "How can you just decide what the final total will be? Don't you have to count the marbles first?"

He smiled and said, "If you count the numbers legitimately, they will always add up to a loser, a number on the chart that carries no points. That's the way the board is designed. If you want to get the mark interested you have to give him some points. So we use the O.C. or over-counting technique." He bent over the board and counted the numbers for me. "Five, eight, eleven, nineteen, twenty-three, and nine is thirty-two. Check thirty-two on the chart."

I found the number on the chart. Underneath the number was printed "5 points." Dad said, "The only way to get that number is for me to count you into it. Let's see what the result would be if I correctly added the numbers." He counted slowly and deliberately, unlike the way he had just reached the previous number. The first time he was counting rapidly, combining marbles and using his fingers in a distracting manner. "That's a legit thirty-four. Find that number on the chart."

I did as instructed and discovered that number to have a blank space underneath, signifying a loser. "That's how it works," he explained. "You let the mark accumulate points at the beginning of the game to get him interested. They never check the addition at the start of the game, only later on when they're hooked and it's too late. It takes many hours of practice to count the numbers before they do. You have to be able to total them correctly with great speed so the mark will trust you. Then you can count him into any number you choose."

Dad looked up and said, "Here comes a mooch now. Look at this guy, he's perfect. Stand back, let me see if I can call him in." I looked down the midway and saw a burly farmer in overalls strolling with his family, a wife in a plain cotton duster and three dirty-faced kids ranging in age from two to six. They looked like they had just come from a barn.

Dad retrieved a bright red card from under the counter and waved it at the farmer as he neared the flat store. On the card was printed the word FREE. "Did you get one of these when you came in the main gate?" he called out. The farmer looked up, somewhat startled. "Are you talking to me?" he inquired.

"Yes," dad said. "There's a midget with a tall red hat handing these out at the entrance." The farmer shook his head as he slowed down in front of the joint.

"We must've come through a different gate. I've been showing my prize hogs. Won a blue ribbon, in fact."

Dad said, "Well then, this is a celebration. Congratulations. You might as well claim your free game now." He held out the card. "This could be your lucky day."

The farmer moved towards him and took the card.

"How's it work?" he asked. "I'll show you," Barry offered helpfully. He pointed to the Razz board and said, "Just exchange that card for a free chance to win a great prize." The farmer moved closer to get a look at the board.

Barry handed him a cup containing eight marbles and said, "Just dump the marbles into the tray and we'll count them up. Then we look on this chart to see if you threw a winner. Ten points is all you need."

The farmer chuckled and said, "Sure, why not. I have nothing to lose." His scruffy family gathered around him. His wife said. "That gold horse clock would look good in our living room." The farmer snorted, "If I win, I'm taking that shotgun on the wall." He looked at Barry and asked, "How do you play this game?"

Dad replied, "I already told you. Just spill the marbles in the cup into the board. Then we'll count them up and see if you hit a winner."

The farmer was still not clear on the rules, but he rolled the marbles anyway. Dad counted them rapidly and announced, "Twenty-two. That's your number." Then he pointed to the chart and added, "Find 22 on that sheet."

The mark studied the chart for a couple of minutes and said, "22 is right here and it says five points. I lose."

Barry responded, "Well it's true you didn't win, but you did pick up five points. If you get another five before you hit a blank you win. It's only fifty cents to play. Give it a try."

The mark looked at his wife and said, "Hey, its only half a dollar. And I might win that shotgun. Whaddaya think?" She shrugged, "I guess." Her husband pulled two quarters from his pocket and handed them over. He rolled the marbles onto the board. Dad then counted them and announced, "Twenty-four. Check that number on the chart."

"Here it is. It says three points. I lose." Barry looked at him and said, "Not exactly. What did you have from before?"

"Five."

"Now what did you get?"'

"Three."

"Five plus three. What does that make?"

"Eight."

"So you now have eight points. What does it take to win?"'

"Ten."

"So you only need two points more to win."

"Only two points?"

"That's right."

"And I can have that shotgun?"

"Absolutely."

The husky farmer looked back at his raggedy family and said, "Hell, I just made $4,200 at the stock auction. I can certainly afford fifty cents to take one more try. If it doesn't work we'll push on down the road." He gave Barry the half-dollar and then emptied the cup of marbles onto the board.

The mention of the large sum of money caused Dad's eyes to light up like he had just seen God. In fact, he had, since money was the closest thing to spiritual enlightenment in his life. He took a deep breath and counted the marbles. They totaled 29. "Twenty-nine," he announced excitedly. "That's the BEST number on the board!"

"It is?" asked the big man. "Where is that on the chart?" He began to scan the sheet intensely. "Oh, there it is. It says H.P. What does that mean?"

"It means House Pays. You are now guaranteed a winner. You haven't hit any blanks yet. If you had, you would have lost all the points you had accumulated. Now, if you hit a blank you get to keep the points you've earned. You can never lose them as long as you play. It also means that the house pays YOU double when you win. Instead of winning one prize you are now playing for your choice of any TWO prizes."

The woman in the frumpy dress and unkempt hair said to her husband, "If you win two, I want that gold horse-clock." Her husband replied, "Why not take the portable radio?" She bowed her head and said, "Whatever you say. But that clock shore is pretty." He reached into his pocket and extracted fifty cents.

Barry said, "You can save your money. H.P. also means the house pays you double what you spent to play. You paid 50 cents so I'm now giving you double or one dollar." He pulled a dollar out of his pocket and placed it in the mark's hand. "Of course, it now costs you double to play, since you're going for TWO great prizes."

The farmer shrugged and handed Barry the dollar back. "I'll try it again." He grinned smugly at his wife and added, "Hey now I'm playing on their money." He emptied the marbles onto the board and Barry counted to 17. "Ah, seventeen, find that on the chart."

The player scanned the sheet and started, "There it is. It says one point." Barry said, "Now if you add that to what you already have...let's see five plus three plus one. Nine points. One more and you take your choice of any two prizes."

The farmer was getting excited. "Ya hear that honey. One point and we get TWO prizes." He pulled out his wallet and extracted a five dollar bill which he handed over. He also gave Barry a chance to observe a fat wad of bills, which carnies call "a peek at the poke." It was enough to get Barry's heart pounding. He changed the five, known on the carnival lot as a "fin" and handed the mark the cup of marbles which he then dumped onto the Razz board.

When he was done counting, Dad announced, "Twenty nine. Twenty-nine? Oh my God, do you remember 29? The best number on the board? H.P. House Pays. Let's see, you paid one dollar to play so I give you double or two dollars. Here take these. Plus, you are now playing for THREE PRIZES when you get one more point." He placed two one dollar bills in the farmer's gnarled fingers. "Of course, it now costs you two dollars to play."

"That's fine. I got two dollars right here." He handed the two bills back to Pop. "Let's play," the farmer said enthusiastically. He emptied the cup of marbles onto the board. Barry counted them up and announced "Forty-two. Find 42 on the chart." The farmer found the number and said dejectedly, "It's a blank. NO points."

Dad said, "That's not a winner. Not yet. You're bound to hit a blank once in awhile. The good news is that you don't lose the nine points you've already accumulated. As soon as you hit for that last point you get your choice of three expensive prizes worth hundreds of dollars."

The mark handed over two more dollars. "I'll try one more time. But this is the last. If I lose, we're leaving." He poured the contents of the cup onto the board and Barry counted them announcing, "Number forty-three. Find 43 on the chart." The farmer scanned the chart for a minute then exclaimed, "One-half point. What does that mean?"

Barry said, "It means that you now have 9 1/2 points. If you notice, a half-point is the smallest number on the chart. Now, when you hit any number with a point on it you win. Anything other than a blank, anything with a positive number you win."

The mark looked a little bewildered. "What if I go over ten points? What happens then? Do I have to hit ten exactly?"'

Barry responded, "No. Ten or more points is a winner. If you go over, you still win. Ya wanna give it one more try? It's still just two bucks to play."

"Sure. Why not? I'm this close. I'll give it another shot." He handed over the money and spilled the marbles. Barry quickly counted and enthusiastically reported, "It's 29 again. The best number on the board. Here's five dollars and you're now playing for FOUR prizes. Of course, it now costs you five to play. Do you want to go on?"

The farmer looked at the five-dollar bill in his hand and said, "Sure, gimme the marbles," as he handed the bill back.

From that time onwards he hits nothing but blanks. Blank, blank, blank. He turned to his wife and said, "Honey, why don't you take the kids on a few rides. I'm gonna finish this game. It might take a little while. But I'm playing for four prizes now; I'll definitely get you that gold horse clock you admire." She nodded obediently and shuttled the children down the midway. "C'mon kids, let's get some cotton candy and check out the rides," she said as they moved away.

The mark was clearly hooked. He was certain that he was only one shot away from collecting hundreds of dollars in prizes. What difference did it make if he spent a hundred or even two hundred? When he hit, he would come out way ahead. And he only needed a half-point or more to win. A virtual cinch, he thought.

I decided it was time to take a walk. When the family left, it was a little obvious for me to be nosing in on the game. Dad and the mark were involved in what appeared to be confidential communication. I decided to treat myself to a corndog. I knew it wasn't good for me but I didn't care. I ate everything. Candy apples, popcorn, corn-on-the-cob and endless burgers.

My all-junk diet changed when we played county fairs with incredible down-home cookin' booths scattered across the fairgrounds; fried chicken to die for, homemade strawberry pies, huge racks of ribs casting fragrant smoke over the tents. During the course of the fair, I hit every farm-fresh dish available.

I was fascinated by the science and industrial exhibits. There were demonstrations of the latest technologies and cutting-edge products soon to be available.

I spent time cruising the livestock pens where blue ribbon animals were placed proudly on display by their owners. The rural atmosphere of the fairs exposed me to a part of life not often seen by city dwellers.

But I was especially drawn to the country fresh young girls who turned out in great numbers. I checked them out while on my breaks and then waited to spot them on the carnival midway. If they passed by my joint, I would strike up a conversation and offer to take one lucky young lady on the ride of her choice. No paying and no waiting.

It was a real magnetic approach which allowed me to get close to the locals, sometimes resulting in a few sweaty moments behind one of the tents. I didn't know anything about sex, but I was discovering how much fun girls could be.

It was about 45 minutes later when I returned to the Count Store where Dad was still playing the farmer. I arrived at the same time as the mark's family. The wife spoke first. "Harold, are you still playing that SAME game?" Her husband, slightly flushed answered, "Yeah. I spent a lot of money and I still ain't won squat."

Barry chimed in, "It only takes one good one to make up for all the bad ones. You've had a string of bad ones. Your luck is bound to change." The woman stepped up to the counter and inquired, "Just how much money have you lost, honey?" The farmer scratched his head and said, "About twenty-six hundred."

His wife looked like she had just been kicked in the stomach by a mule. "Dollars?" she asked.

"Yep, but things have changed. I'm now playing for eight prizes. I can clean this place out as soon as I score a half-point.

And this feller here says that he'll buy back any or all of 'em for $500 a piece."

She nearly slumped to the ground. "Twenty-six hundred dollars! That's over half the money we got to last us through the winter." She began to cry. The kids looked on wide-eyed, not fully comprehending the situation, and never having seen their mother in tears before.

"It's okay, honey. As soon as I get a winner we're gonna have all of our money back plus a couple of prizes."

She sobbed louder, "I don't give a damn about any prizes. How are we going to live when the snows come and we're out of money?"

The farmer said, "Whyn't you take the kids for a burger? I'll join you shortly."

"You mean you're gonna continue to play?" she cried out incredulously. "How could you?"

"I gotta get even. I can't leave when I'm this close to winning."

The woman shot him a glance of sheer malevolence. She shuffled the kids off towards the burger joint. "I'll see you in ten minutes, no more," she stated flatly as they left.

Barry said to the farmer, "She seems really upset. You sure you want to continue?" I didn't realize it at the time, but dad was trying to "cool the mark" or get him to quit. He didn't want to take any more of the farmer's money for fear that the wife would make a big stink and he might have to kick back some, or all, of the big score.

But the farmer was having none of it. "I come this far. I ain't quittin' now. Gimme the marbles. Here's your two hundred."

I was impressed. The guy was paying two hundred dollars per game. It was unthinkable in my world. Barry took the cash and said, "Well, then, jolly good luck to you. I hope you win." The mark spilled the marbles onto the board and Barry counted them up. It came up a blank. A loser. "Seems like you just hit a long string of blanks. Maybe your luck has run out," he said.

The farmer was turning beet red. There was a definite sense of impending violence in the air. He said, "Ya know, it's awfully strange that I got all those points in the beginning and I can't git anythin' now. It almost seems like this game is fixed."

Barry responded, "It can't be fixed. No one can control which slots the marbles fall in. It's pure luck." The farmer considered this comment a moment then reached into his pocket for money to try again. Barry was getting very concerned and said, "You've been a really good customer so I have a suggestion. Let me pay for this game."

"Thanks," said the mark and dumped the marbles onto the board. Barry counted him into a 29, which added a prize but also doubled the cost of each game. The carny then said, "Another H.P. so I pay you double. Here's $400. Now, however, it costs you $400 per game to play."

"I do have another suggestion. If you want to end the game now I will trade you the 9 1/2 points you've accumulated for that shotgun you have your eye on and the gold horse clock for your wife, just because you're such a good sport."

The farmer considered the proposition and realized that he could only pay for a few more games anyway. This way he might be able to save face and salvage something. "I guess so," he said haltingly.

With great relief, Barry lifted the shotgun off of its rack and set it on the counter. He placed the horse clock next to it and added, "Just because I like you so much, I'm going to include a teddy bear and two poodles for your kids."

In a matter of moments, the mark was laden down with so many prizes he could barely carry them. As he made his way towards the burger stand where his family was eating, Barry shouted out so all could hear, "And there goes another BIG WINNER!"

When he was gone, I asked dad why he stopped the game while the mark was still hot to play. He said, "You have to judge each player carefully. You don't want any grumbling from a hot mark. And you never, ever, take his last money. The shotgun cost me $150.00 four years ago and the horse clock was $49.50. Each piece of plush prices out at $22.50. So for about $250.00 in stock I was able to cool out a play that netted me almost three grand. Do the math."

Settling In

Although my parents had become addicted to heroin well before we moved to the projects, they managed to keep it hidden from us kids. No longer. Our house was now "connection central" for the local junkies. Barry had gone into business with a vengeance. He scored downtown, brought the dope home, cut it and sold it. He added enough sugar to the junk to make a profit. Then he used the profit to shoot more dope.

Mom was another case altogether. She never liked the drug. She tried it because the old man and his friends encouraged her to give it a try. She declined for a long time. Finally, her curiosity led her to give it a shot, so to speak. She didn't like the experience, but she tried it again to see what she was missing. She didn't like it the second time either, or the third.

By that time, she was duped into the addiction. She needed the drug to feel normal. She wound up getting hooked on a substance she abhorred. It was the ultimate irony . . . living the life of an addict, never having experienced the euphoria of the narcotic high in the first place.

Their addiction became full blown once we moved into the Gardens. They were both hooked to the ass. Every day started with a fix to get going and the rest of the day devoted to connecting, cutting and dealing. And, of course, shooting up. The dope engulfed their entire lives.

To complicate matters, my new little sister, just a few months old, was still recovering from the effects of her own withdrawal from the addiction she was born with. Since my mother concealed her own habit so carefully, she was not about to tell the doctors what was wrong with her newborn baby, now known as "Cookie."

Neither Faye nor Barry had given a moment's thought to naming her. They had more important things to do. As a result, the birth certificate simply stated "female, Kahn." They never did get around to giving her a formal name until she enrolled in school at age five. By that time, the little girl had a mind of her own and insisted that "Cookie" be affixed to her birth certificate—and so it was.

Due to the physical withdrawal symptoms my sister had to deal with, there was a constant commotion around her. It was nearly impossible for her to get comfortable, thrashing about in her crib, trying to escape the pain that would not go away. Unlike Mom and Dad, she had to quit "cold turkey." As a result, she cried constantly, keeping everyone on edge.

In our first month in the projects, neighborhood kids threw a rock through the window, spit into my sister's baby carriage, stole my bike, and beat up my brother six times. Our family pet, the duck Squeeky Mae, was kicked repeatedly by passersby and we were forced to find her a new home.

Gang members stalked the area. Gang graffiti was everywhere. The Ramona Gardens projects were the exclusive turf of the "Big Hazard" gang. Nobody messed with them. Even the cops were afraid to come into the projects after dark.

I sought refuge in books and in school. I discovered a whole world of literature out there that recorded everything anybody had ever thought or did, and I wanted to read it all. New worlds opened up to me. I especially liked stories about ordinary kids my age who got an opportunity to be sports heroes on their school teams. I could imagine myself hitting the winning home run or scoring the last-second touchdown.

I loved fiction. There were countless intriguing books springing from the fertile imaginations of dreamers and storytellers—tales of adventure and struggle. Dickens was one of my favorites since his characters had to struggle against the odds, but I primarily engaged in random reading. I would read anything. Books of short stories were great because you could read one complete story on the john from beginning to end.

I was amazed to discover such a wide range of subjects that people had studied and written about. Other times, other places and different types of people drew my attention. The school library was my safe haven. I wandered through the stacks selecting whatever publication my hand happened to land on and stood there reading until I felt like moving on. Sometimes I would sit on the floor between stacks with an armful of periodicals. I read articles from everywhere – women's fashion magazines, the *Saturday Evening Post*, *Sport-*

ing News, you name it.

I could recite the starting lineups of every team in the National League. I knew the batting averages of the top ten hitters in both leagues and the L.A. Rams starting lineup, offense and defense.

I memorized the capitols of every state and the names of every country in the world. I read biographies with great enthusiasm. I wanted to know the life stories of Thomas Edison, Benjamin Franklin, Abraham Lincoln as well as sports heroes like Red Grange, Babe Ruth and Jackie Robinson. I loved stories of people who overcame the odds to achieve greatness. Tales concerning the strength of the human spirit gave me encouragement to deal with the maniacs who happened to be my parents and the surroundings I had to deal with daily. In my imagination, I could see myself as being only temporarily trapped in my living situation. I never doubted for a moment that one day I would move beyond the bounds of my current circumstances. I wasn't sure how or when it would happen, but I knew my day would come.

Confirmation

I decided to find a Hebrew school to finish training for my confirmation. It wasn't that I cared a damn about a bar mitzvah, but I wanted to complete what I started. It gave me one more reason NOT to go home. I never considered attending Hebrew school a religious act. Organized religion of any sort seemed ridiculous to me. I remembered reading somewhere that our greatest president, Abraham Lincoln, was once asked by a reporter about his religion. Abe replied, "When I do bad, I feel bad. When I do good, I feel good. That's my religion." I could live with that.

I found an old orthodox synagogue in the City Terrace neighborhood, not far from the projects. It was a remnant of an earlier day in L.A.'s history when Jewish immigrants settled in the Boyle Heights district of East L.A. Their kids went to Roosevelt High School.

In its heyday, Brooklyn Avenue was the center of the borscht belt, with delicatessens, temples and a vibrant street life. In the years after the war, the Jews began an exodus to West L.A. The Breed Street Temple closed its doors for good. The neighborhood slid into urban slum. Only a few old Jews remained. And their days were numbered by the time I arrived.

There was something compelling about the aging synagogue I had discovered. It was heavy and silent. Ghosts reverberated from the dank, cracked walls. It was pervaded by a smell so unique that it can only be produced by the gathering of observant Jews over decades in a dark, cavernous building, clutching holy books, uttering timeless words and chanting for hours at a time. It was the Old Hebrew aroma.

But there were not many old Hebrews, aside from the Rabbi who taught the bar mitzvah class, consisting of four students. We met in the basement of the temple in the only room still in use in the entire building. There were still services in the main room on the High Holidays and a surprising number of people showed up. We were most likely the last bar mitzvah class that would be offered.

Because I never wanted to go home, I showed up for

Hebrew class early and stayed late. I often found myself sitting alone inside the ancient house of worship doing my school assignments. It was peaceful. It was quiet. I felt safe. The Rabbi mistakenly thought I was an unusually dedicated student of the *Torah*, not someone just seeking refuge from the rest of his life.

I liked being the only one present. It was as though this great edifice were constructed just for me to do my homework in the afternoons. It was the only break in my day when I got to be alone. For the first time in my life I was glad I was Jewish. It was paying off.

It paid off in cash as well. The Rabbi introduced me to Mr. Solovsky who owned a butcher shop nearby. He needed a boy for after-school deliveries. I jumped at the opportunity. He provided a bicycle for the job and I loved to ride. Making money for biking around the neighborhood seemed like an easy way to earn spending cash. It was a fun job. I got to know all the local streets intimately, as well as our regular customers who got to know me and sometimes threw me a tip. I liked tips.

I needed money for clothes, transportation, movies, tacos, records and for just about everything else except air. Then I used my pay from my delivery job to buy a second hand lawn mower and used edger. I went door to door on the weekends with my little brother, pushing my tools from apartment to apartment. Each living area had a postage stamp sized green patch in the front yard. I had a flexible fee schedule which depended on how much cash they were willing to spend. I would take anything from fifty cents down to a dime. Some I did for free because they had no money.

Rich Relatives

A couple of times a year, we went to visit Dad's family, all of whom lived in Beverly Hills or Bel Air. Three of his sisters had found their way to L.A. and had married well. Aunt Lil did the best. Her husband Marcel was a successful optometrist with an office in the Broadway department store downtown. They and their twin girls lived in the hills above Sunset Blvd. in a magnificent estate.

I went there only one time because they had a superior attitude that prevented them from socializing with our motley crew. The twins treated me like dirt, not even worthy of their disdain. Aunt Lillian, who reminded me of Joan Crawford at her nastiest, always looked like she smelled something bad when she saw us. Uncle Marcel, however, was a genuinely well-intentioned man. He was unfortunately bulldozed by his wife and daughters. We seldom saw them except at Aunt Edith's house, a beautiful spread down on the flatlands of Beverly Hills.

Dad's sister Edith had married Gordon Levoy, a successful lawyer and a big shot in the Beverly Hills Jewish community. For some reason, Aunt Edith tolerated our occasional visits. They had three kids about our age. Larry was the eldest, then Linda, and last was the baby, Lola. The contrast between their lives and ours could not be greater.

Aunt Bobby, whose husband had passed away, lived on the edges of Beverly Hills, thanks to the generosity of her sisters. Her son Michael was about my age and I had grown up with him.

I remember driving up to the Levoy's stately two-story home on Maple Drive on a Sunday afternoon one spring day in 1954. We had visited the great home a number of times in the past. I knew the entire layout by memory. The exquisitely furnished interior led to a spacious back yard which was a fully equipped recreation area, complete with a built-in brick barbecue and enough room to entertain dozens of people in style.

Their home was something out of a Hollywood movie and never ceased to amaze me. It was hard for me to grasp that people actually lived that way.

Our beat-up '39 Plymouth shitbox was totally out of place in the luxurious setting. We parked on the street in front of the house and made an attempt to be as inconspicuous as possible, but it was a futile effort since the car was backfiring and emitting a cloud of black smoke that announced our arrival to the entire neighborhood. I was also well aware of the oil leak that was going to leave a black puddle when we departed. I was embarrassed but there was nothing I could do.

Inside the house, I could imagine Uncle Gordon, clad in his smoking jacket, and Aunt Edith, fashionably chic, peeking from behind heavy drapes and sharing their loathing for the newly arrived visitors. Gordon would be saying, "Oh no, it's your good-for-nothing brother and his whole circus act. I hope you didn't invite him."

I could see him looking at her accusingly, his wife replying, "Of course, I didn't invite them. They just showed up. Maybe they won't stay long."

Then Gordon would say, "I hope you're right about that. In and out, please. I'll say hello, then retire to the library. Call me when they leave."

We entered the house, and I felt transported into some fantasy depiction of life in the upper classes. Everything was clean and well cared for. The maid puttered around the kitchen preparing goodies for the family and, now unexpected visitors. Then I looked up to the balcony where my adorable cousin Linda leaned over and called out to Aunt Edith. "I'm done with my homework, mother" she said. "Can I come down now?"

Auntie scurried upstairs and entered her eldest daughter's room to determine whether the homework assignment was truly and accurately completed. When she had satisfied herself that all was done properly, she returned to the living room with Linda in hand. I was stunned by my cousin's innocent beauty. I was frozen speechless in her presence and so went outside to play ping pong to avoid having to deal with my overwhelming feelings.

Uncle Gordon strode elegantly across the living room looking very important with his pipe clenched between his teeth. In a matter of moments, he disappeared into his inner sanctum, closing the door behind him, not to be seen again until we departed. He spoke sparingly and, over the years never said a word to me. In all the times we visited their house, I cannot remember a single exchange.

"What does Uncle Gordon do?" I asked Mom. She replied, "He's a lawyer." I wanted to know more. "What do lawyers do?" I inquired. She answered, "They go around saying important things and get paid very well for it." I was dumbfounded. "That's it? Just talk and get lots of money?" Mom smiled, "As far as I can tell."

I made the decision right then and there. I was going to be a lawyer and have a giant house in Beverly Hills, smoke a pipe, say important things and make lots of money.

I knew my rich relatives had no idea what kind of life we were living. Nor did they care. No one ever asked any questions or showed the slightest interest in my family. We were outsiders who were intruding into their well-ordered world. We were barely tolerated and they made little effort to disguise their desire to have us gone.

While part of me wanted to remain in that house forever, it was a great relief to get out of there. It was a bit creepy. My relatives were not like real human beings. They were more like bad actors playing upper crust jerks. I never could figure out why they didn't seem happy. They had everything.

When we drove off, I noticed the pool of oil that the shitbox had deposited on the immaculate street. It seemed to make a statement, but I wasn't sure what it was. I was certain that it was nothing good.

Cookie for Sale

By late spring of l954, the situation at home was getting desperate. Although the rent on our three bedroom apartment was only $35 per month, we fell behind and began receiving eviction notices. I realized that the next step down was living on the streets. There was no way to talk to my parents about the impending doom because of their all-encompassing addiction. Every dollar went into the glory hole in their arms. There was nothing left for rent or even food.

We had begun to run a tab at Abe's Market, the only commercial establishment in the projects. Abe, who ran the store with the help of his grown son, had a soft spot in his heart for the newborn baby girl Mom would bring along on shopping trips. He also saw an opportunity to put a move on Faye. She was desperate to feed her family and he knew it.

As the debt grew, he became increasingly bold in his approach. One day at the checkout counter Abe said, "So, I expect you want more credit. Maybe we can work out a deal to wipe out your debt and give you some money as well." Mom looked at him inquisitively and asked, "What do you have in mind?"

Abe answered, "I think your baby is too much trouble for you. You can't even afford to feed her. My wife and I could give her a good home and see that she is well cared for, and you could get a nice chunk of cash as well."

Mom was stunned. "You want me to SELL you my baby? You must be nuts." Abe tried to pacify her. "You should think about the child. She would have a better life with us. We can give her the things she needs. We would provide her with everything."

"Everything but her mother. How would you give her a mother's love and care?" Faye retorted. "You must be out of your mind to think for one minute that I would just give her to you."

Abe replied, "It's not a gift. I would pay you well. Thousands of dollars. With that kind of money, you could afford to move to a decent neighborhood and give your two sons a real chance in life. They're nice boys. You should think of their future. You don't want them to become gangsters in this hellhole."

Mom was angry, but she was listening. If Abe cut off her credit, there would be no food in the house. She said, "Well you can just forget about it. Just as a matter of curiosity, how much would you be willing to pay?"

Abe sensed her weakening. "Oh, maybe four, five thousand, in cash. But you would have to agree to a legal adoption." He had obviously been thinking about this deal for some time. He watched closely for her reaction.

She snatched up the groceries and said, "Thanks for your kind offer, but I don't think so. If I change my mind I'll let you know."

She left the market, her head spinning. The baby was very young and had not really bonded with the family yet. "No, no, it's impossible," she thought. Part of her wanted to say "Yes," and move out of this crummy, roach-infested project. She finally decided the best thing to do was to go home and shoot up, becoming blissfully unaware of her surroundings for a short time.

I didn't know what to think. I wanted out desperately. I wanted my old life back. I hated being frightened twenty-four hours a day. I hated the gangs, the graffiti, and the ever-present cockroaches. But no one ever asked for my input, so I kept my feelings to myself. In truth, I probably would have been happy to trade my little sister for a life of sanity.

The Bar Mitzvah

In June, I celebrated my 13th birthday in the confines of the old orthodox synagogue, chanting my Haftorah, a long and difficult recitation in Hebrew. Only my family attended the service. None of my other relatives would even consider coming to East L.A. for any reason. A few people scattered throughout the temple heard the performance and the mandatory speech thereafter in which I thanked the Rabbi, my parents, my teachers and everyone else on the face of the earth.

There was a party later at my Uncle Nate's house. Mom's entire family had migrated west from Philly following her example. They were much more accepting of our brood than Dad's snobby sisters, and invited the entire clan to get together regularly. That occasion was as close as we ever got to being a real family. Three generations of offspring from the immigrant couple from Russia and Poland gathered in honor of me, Kenny, becoming a man. It was my moment to shine. I was the star. And everyone was there.

Uncle Nate's place was located in the far reaches of the San Fernando Valley, in a new town called Sherman Oaks. It was one of the first neighborhoods to offer affordable housing to white people fleeing the inner city. He purchased a home for his family, which consisted of his wife, Sirry, whom he had first met in McArthur Park many years earlier, and his two girls, Arlyne, age 12, whom he called Wiggles, and 10-year old Tina, known as Poochie.

Her oldest brother, Herman, or Steve as he was now known, had married his childhood sweetheart, the diminutive Esther. Steve looked successful with a ruddy, healthy complexion, a full bristling black moustache and a pronounced paunch. He had a jovial exterior, but inside he was definitely his father's son. He was a professional middle-man, selling someone else's products to retailers. He had a stubborn streak that caused him to bark orders every now and then. It was pretty clear he ought to be obeyed, or else. He was offset by his wife, Aunt Esther, a fashion plate and upper-class wannabe. A slight woman with big glasses, she was appropriately polite to everyone. They had gone together as teenagers back in Philly, eventually married and had an only child, my eleven-year old cousin, Bonnie, a mini-Esther in the making. Only her youth made her less obnoxious.

Faye's older sister, Sally, who was rapidly becoming mentally unbalanced, was present with her henpecked, docile husband, George, the only non-Jew in the group, and her two children, 19-year-old Donald, the only sane one whom I looked up to, and her young daughter, Terry Lee who slept on the couch.

Even detested Grandpa Philip showed up with the latest of his five wives, the first four of whom were acquired for financial reasons and then discarded after their money ran out. Number five still had some bucks so he tolerated her. Although he had been eighty-sixed from the family home nearly twenty years earlier, he had managed a reconciliation and was once again part of the family. He smelled vaguely similar to the old synagogue and wore a shirt with chicken soup stains. He still sounded like he had just gotten off the boat from Poland, with a thick Yiddish accent.

The only non-family member attending was Barry's carny pal Paul Hoffman, a would-be screenwriter, who had also come to the service in the synagogue that morning. He gave me my only bar mitzvah gift, a hard-bound collegiate dictionary.

We gathered in the spacious back yard which featured a portable rubber swimming pool, acquired from Uncle Nate's current employer, "Doughboy." It wasn't like a real pool, but you could splash around and hold your cousin's head under water. It was a hot day in the valley and the cool water was perfect.

Uncle Nate was a good-natured guy who liked to provide the setting for his family's get-togethers. Clean shaven, he had a pleasant face with a ready smile. But, like his older brother Steve, there was a streak of the Brody evil side running through him. Mostly he was a pussycat, but then he could become extremely unreasonable at any moment. It seemed like a power thing to me. This was HIS party and HE was doing the entertaining.

The reason he could entertain so well was his wife, Sirry.

She had a homespun welcoming personality that made everyone feel comfortable. She cared, deeply and sincerely, about her guests' wishes, wants and needs. She had a warm smile and made everyone feel special.

She was the only adult who asked me questions like how I was doing in school, did I have a girlfriend, and how did I like having a new baby sister. She sat down with me one-on-one in a back bedroom and talked about my life like no one else did. There was an uncommon kindness to her. She was also the glue that kept us all together, even though we were only her family through marriage. Sally was too crazy to host a large affair and Esther couldn't be bothered. Faye certainly wasn't about to invite the gang to the housing project. So that left Sirry to do the heavy lifting. Luckily, she was happy to do it.

We splashed away the hot summer afternoon in the pool. Their rambunctious little dog, Nugget, dashed around the yard playing with the kids. The adults sat in the shade kibitzing and playing pinochle. Aunt Sirry, Aunt Esther, and the Brody girls chattered like mad in the kitchen, while preparing the bar mitzvah feast. Grandpa and his newest squeeze sat at the dining room table talking about whatever old Jews talk about.

My only regret was that grandma Tillie was not there. She had moved from Strawberry Mansion in Philadelphia to Ocean Park a couple of years after Mom and Dad. She doted on me when I was an infant, pushing my stroller down the boardwalk and showing me off to the old Jews who populated the benches by the sand.

My only images of her were from old, yellowing photos taken in the last years before her death. Her life had changed dramatically from the horrible years suffered under Philip's thumb in Philly. She had learned English in her later years and become a social creature.

In the pictures taken of her holding me, she was beaming from ear to ear. It was easy to see the pleasure she took in my young life. I missed her, desperately.

Donald was the oldest of my cousins. At nineteen, he was clearly at a different stage of development than the rest of us younger kids. He was my role model. He was good looking, had a driver's license, and he proudly wore the uniform of the United States Air Force.

When we were living in West Adams, he had arranged for me to go to work selling Sunday newspapers outside a Catholic church. He picked me up at five a.m. on Sunday morning, drove me to the church, deposited me and my papers on the corner and split. He returned after the last mass to pick me up. In between, I was on my own. I soon discovered that no one buys the paper going INTO the church.

After the service I was inundated with business. Everyone wanted a paper on the way home and I was bombarded for fifteen minutes. Then it was dead again for the next 45 minutes. Instead of standing in the cold of the early daylight, I took refuge inside the church. It was warm. I was happy. Some days I attended three masses. It was better than standing in the street shivering.

Cousin Donald was too young to relate to the adults and too old to play with the kids. He compromised by going back and forth during the afternoon, spending time in both camps. I learned a lot from him. He taught me what a negligee was. My hero.

The late afternoon sun was setting when my big moment arrived.

The tables were festively decorated and ready for dinner. The entire family gathered in the backyard for my monumental moment of recognition. The outdoor lights were activated. Uncle Nate stepped forward and announced, "Ladies and gentlemen, we are gathered here today to recognize that our boy, Kenny, is today no longer a boy but a Man." A round of applause. "I now have the distinct pleasure of introducing Kenny who will recite the speech he gave in the synagogue this morning." More applause.

I nervously repeated my earlier speech thanking everyone in the universe for their help. It seemed hopelessly out of place in this suburban setting but I pressed on nonetheless. I had to. I was a man.

Then it was over. In a flash, all the months of my preparation, study and rehearsal were now finished. Kaput. Done. Toast. My moment in the spotlight was truly just a moment. The next minute, they were much more interested in the antics of Nugget, the dog and the status of the barbecue. I realized that fame was fleeting, and it had done fled. My first lesson as a "Man."

After dinner, all the cousins except for Donald retired to a corner of the house to write a play which we would later perform for the adults. Since I was the oldest boy, I got to play the male lead. My 12-year old cousin Arlyne and my 11-year old cousin Bonnie fought over the female lead. Ten-year old Tina and my brother, nine-year old Ricki, were assigned the bit parts.

We developed a script which called for me to be king. Both Arlyne and Bonnie decided to be the queens. I was aware that there should be only ONE queen, but in the interest of keeping the peace we had two.

The script was not written down. We created only the broad outlines of the story. As king, I had just returned from a successful campaign in which I vanquished the enemy. There was to be a great victory celebration. Tina was allowed to be the princess just to keep her from complaining that she never got a good part. Ricki was to be the court jester. He knew one song and would be allowed to sing it.

The actual storyline was intentionally vague, giving each of us an opportunity to add whatever struck us at the time. We never knew what was going to happen until we took the stage. The parents didn't care and pretended to be enormously entertained no matter what we did.

The play was greeted with applause as we entered the stage, which was the living room floor. Each actor received individual hurrahs as they began to speak their lines. The adults were obviously enjoying themselves as they downed after-dinner coffee and dessert. Few of them paid any attention to what was actually being said. More important was how "cute" we were. That part was easy to live up to. Parents, like parents everywhere, beamed with pride at the mere sight of their precious offspring appearing on stage and blowing lines.

As usual, the play drew a tremendous ovation as the curtain closed. The actors were filled with self-satisfied congratulations and each secretly dreamed of the day they would be discovered by Hollywood. Meanwhile we retired to the back room for milk and sweets. Each of us was greatly satisfied with our performance.

Our celebration was suddenly halted when Uncle Steve opened the door wearing a very serious expression. "Come here," he said to me an a low and ominous voice. "Now."

I stepped into the hallway where I saw a crowd of aunts, uncles and grandparents gathered outside the bathroom. They were buzzing about something happening on the other side of the closed bathroom door. There was a look of great concern on each of their faces. "Your dad passed out on the bathroom floor," Uncle Nate said. "Your mom's in there with him now. Do you know what's wrong with him?" They all looked at me, expectantly.

"Yes, I do," I said, reaching for the door handle, turning it, and entering. Outside the door I could hear cackling voices. "We should call a doctor." "At this hour? What doctor is coming out at this hour? You know someone?" "Not here. In Philadelphia we had someone." "Forget Philadelphia. We live here now. What good is Philadelphia here? Here is where we have a problem, not Philadelphia." "So call an ambulance." "To take him where?" "To the hospital." "Which hospital?" "I dunno. Has he got insurance?" "Barry? You got to be kidding. He doesn't know from insurance." "Well, we've got to get him some help, anyway." "So YOU call the ambulance, Mr. Big Shot. You can afford hospitals? Go on, call."

Dad was sprawled out on the bathroom floor, drooling, his eyes rolled back into his head, which was being cradled in Mom's lap. She had tears in her eyes. "He snuck away from the party while everyone was watching the play. He came in here and fixed. He must have gotten some bad shit. I don't know what to do."

His face revealed no noticeable sign of life. He could be dead or just unconscious. I said, "Why don't we try to get him on his feet. Let's stand him up." We each took an arm and a shoulder and propped him up. He was dead weight, but luckily didn't weigh much. Like most junkies, he was all skin and bones. We stood still holding him upright for a few minutes while discussing what to do next. We decided to hold his head under the tap in the sink. I turned on the water and Mom began to splash his face.

He started to slump to the ground so we bent him over the bathtub and stuck his head directly under the cold water tap. I turned it on full tilt. His eyelashes began to flutter and he let out a discernable breath. He wasn't done yet. He would live to shoot up another day.

When we laid him back down he was breathing easily. Mom went to her family and explained that everything was all right but he would need a bed for the night. Uncle Nate agreed and Barry was brought to a bedroom and snugly tucked in, oblivious to the anxiety and confusion he left in his wake.

Once he was safely out of the way, all hell broke loose in the living room. Uncle Nate worried, "I still think we should call a doctor. What if he dies here? Then what?" Mom responded, "He's OK now. He just needs a good night's sleep. He'll be fine in the morning." Sally chimed in, "How can you be so sure? He could die, you know. You're not God."

Her goy husband, George nodded in agreement. That was about as animated as George ever got. Steve added his two cents, "What's his problem, anyway? Has he got some sort of a secret disease?" His wife Esther chimed in, "Steve's right. Barry looked bad when he got here this afternoon and he's gone steadily downhill since."

Grandpa Phil, sitting on the loveseat with his new wife who was now snoring softly on his shoulder, added, "I never trusted him. I shouldn't have let Fannie marry him."

Nate said, "Can it Pop. You haven't had anything to say about how any of us live our lives for twenty years." His wife, Sirry, smiled and added helpfully, "But that doesn't mean we don't all still love you, Poppy."

The kids were informed that we would not be going home that evening. There would be a shifting of sleeping arrangements to allow our family to stay in the valley.

I spent that night in my girl cousins' bedroom with my little brother. The girls migrated to another bedroom in which they immediately started a pillow fight with the dog.

I was exhausted. It had been a long time since the service in the synagogue that morning. I was happy to crawl into bed. I closed my eyes and looked forward to a peaceful night. Before I could sleep, Aunt Sirry came into the darkened bedroom carrying something in her hand. It was a dish with orange slices arranged carefully in a semi-circle. She pulled a chair up to the bedside and placed the dish on it. "In case you get thirsty in the middle of the night," she said. She kissed me lightly on the forehead and left the room.

I was dumbfounded. Nobody had ever cared about me getting thirsty in the middle of the night! It was outside my understanding of how people behave. It was the greatest act of kindness anyone had ever shown me. I couldn't believe that someone cared about my comfort level in the middle of the night. I felt tears begin to well up in my eyes. I slept blissfully through the night. The orange slices went untouched.

The Family Hits the Road

That summer we hit the road as an entire family entity. The baby was old enough to travel. Mom was dying to get out of the "stinking projects" and we could be together as a family. We constituted a full-on carnival troupe.

Dad operated the flat store and made the big money. I played a hanky pank and did fairly well. My 10-year old brother ran errands for the carnies, acted as a shill, and helped me steal money from my boss. Mom sold tickets to the thrill rides. Only Cookie, the baby, didn't do much of anything.

We were hooked up with West Coast Shows and scheduled to play the entire northwest from upper California to the Canadian border, and beyond. We were set to split from the show at the end of the season to jump up to British Columbia for the massive Pacific National Exhibition, or PNE as it was known. The fair was so huge and so lucrative, it was said a carny could live the entire winter from money earned at the PNE alone.

We started out playing the farming communities in the middle of the San Joaquin Valley and worked our way up north. Eventually the show set up on the Redding, California fairgrounds. For some inexplicable reason, the actual location of the Shasta County Fair was in Anderson, 10 miles from the main town of Redding. Either way, it was rustic northern California at its best, with lots of trees and farmland.

Since there were no accommodations in Anderson itself, we headquartered in Redding making the 20 mile roundtrip commute each day. I didn't mind. We were all together as a family and out of Ramona Gardens for the summer, away from the gangs, graffiti, and junkies who inhabited our house.

Since Barry could not score heroin in this part of the country, he switched to prescription drugs.

The carnies had a "croaker" in every town the show played. He was a local doctor who would write prescriptions for anything the carnies wanted—for a price. Dad would go into the office, explain that he had a narcotics addiction and needed something to help him deal with his withdrawal symptoms. He came away with several scripts for heavy duty morphine-based products. His favorite was doliphene, or 'dollies' as they were known. He also acquired Doridin and Codeine #4 which would be taken together and were known as 'doors and fours.' In this way, he could work and stay loaded at the same time.

Each day, the fair did not get underway full tilt until sunset. Then the crowds would arrive in numbers. Mom had found a perfect job for a lady with a baby, selling tickets to the roller coaster ride.

She sat on a stool with the baby on her lap inside a darkened booth with a dense metal grating where a window should be. The construction of this booth was not an accident. It was impossible to see clearly through the opaque screen. When a customer was due change, Mom would slide part of the money through the opening at the bottom of the cage. The balance would be discreetly placed to the rear. If the customer did not count their money, she would pocket the balance. It was a slick scam. Most people boarding a thrill ride were not very interested in counting change. They were distracted by the noise, the excitement, and the prospect of getting on the roller coaster.

Occasionally a mark would inquire about the rest of his change. Mom would simply say, "It's right here. Look through the cash opening." The mark would then bend down to peer inside the opening and, lo and behold, there was his change just sitting there. "Oh, sorry, I didn't see it," was the most common response.

Ricki made himself useful going from joint to joint inquiring whether any of the agents needed anything from the refreshment stands. When things got busy, he did a good business in tips. In between, he worked as a "stick" or "shill," winning prizes and walking around with them, then depositing them in the back of the joint from which it was taken. Each joint slipped him a few bucks.

My little brother served as my partner in crime. When he ran errands for me while I was working, I gave him money for the food and drink I wanted plus I slipped him an extra fin, five dollars, or a sawbuck, ten dollars, or sometimes if things were going really well a double, 20 bucks. This was a convenient way for me to steal money from my apron without causing suspicion. Stuffing money directly into your pocket was dangerous because you could be spotted. If challenged, the crumpled cash could be used as evidence against you. It was much cleaner this way.

After closing time, we all returned to our motel to wash up before going to a late night breakfast. The entire family would dump the proceeds from the day onto the bed and count it up. It looked like a treasure trove with piles of bills and coins scattered over the chenille bedspread. We had more money than we needed. We were rich. Yahoo!

For the time being, it was easy to forget that in September the party would be over and we would have to go back to survive public housing. For now, we could afford to stay at good motels with a swimming pool, eat at the best places, and have plenty of spending cash on hand.

Another thing I had was plenty of spare time. There are long stretches during every fair when things are slow. I stuck my nose in everywhere. I watched cattle-judging shows, hog-breeding demonstrations, prize-winning horses, and some of the world's healthiest fruits and vegetables displayed in great array in huge show halls. You could taste blue-ribbon cherry pie. It was as Americana as it gets. These citizens were downhome, honest, tillers of the soil who had produced harvests of plenty.

Seeing them provided me with a startling contrast to the seedy carnival life. These were simply hard-working people who labored from dawn to dusk. They raised their families and asked for nothing. They earned everything they had. There was no sham. No flim-flam. No gaff. Just plain, unvarnished, back-breaking physical labor. I was amazed. I couldn't believe people lived that way. It seemed like a constantly challenging, sweaty way to get by. But it exuded health and simplicity. There was something very attractive in that. I wondered what my life would have been like had I been raised in this setting.

Side Shows

That summer, the carnival was livened up with a combination of freak acts known as side shows. They had their own giant tent which housed the various attractions including The Fat Lady, the baby with two heads, Mr. Tattoo, and most intriguing to me, the Girlie show, known as Fatima and the Harem. As a 13- year old, I was excluded by my tender age from buying a ticket to the show, but as a carny I was welcome to wander in and out of the employees' entrance freely.

There was a raised platform about fifty feet long set up in front of the side-show tent. A barker wearing a spiffy red suit, a straw hat and carrying a gold cane had the job of attracting a crowd. He had a microphone stand set up in the center of the outdoor stage from which he could address the fairgoers and attempt to entice them to buy a ticket to the show.

He began his spiel in a loud and excited voice. "Step right up, gentlemen. The next show is one you'll want to catch while your wives are busy watching the children on the kiddie rides. Yesiree, we are about to explore the exotic forbidden pleasures of the Middle East. The world renown mistress of sensuality, Fatima, will set your blood boiling."

A few men stopped for a moment to listen to what the guy on the stage had to say. "Before you rush to buy a ticket, I must warn you that Fatima's erotic Snake Dance, with a real live snake, is not for everyone. If you have a weak heart, I recommend the Merry-go-Round. More than one gentleman has been carried out of her show feet first." The crowd began to swell from a scattered few to a full on throng.

"And now, an absolutely free taste of what awaits you under the big top." Middle Eastern music began to roll up from the speakers placed at opposite ends of the stage. "The Goddess Fatima has graciously consented to permit two of her harem slave girls to join me here on the stage to delight your senses. C'mon up close. You'll want to get a real good look." As the crowd pressed forward, a bare leg with silver

137

bangles slid out from behind a curtain strategically located behind the barker.

"Remember, this is for adults only." He turned to a youngster straining to see under the curtain and said, "Stand back, sonny. You'll have to get your thrills from National Geographic." The crowd began to laugh as the embarrassed lad tried to sneak away.

From behind the curtain, two average looking, heavily made-up women in belly-dancing garb shuffled ungracefully across the stage. The onlookers were aroused nonetheless. The girls did a brief hoochy-koo, shaking what they had in time with the music. This elicited much hooting and hollering from the crowd which was by now quite sizeable.

"And that's just the beginning, my friends. Inside you will experience the thrill of a lifetime. Step right up. Tickets are now on sale for the next show. ONLY TWO BUCKS. Who'll be first?"

An old man in the back cried out, "I will," while waving two singles in the air. Suddenly, a hand reached out and snagged his arm. The hand was attached to a matronly woman, obviously his wife. "Oh no, you won't. You're coming with me, you little weasel." The crowd loved it and resumed hooting and hollering, then began to move towards the ticket booth at the entrance to the tent as she hauled him off.

I walked around to the back of the tent and found a rear employee's entrance. I slipped in, unnoticed, I thought. Half a dozen girls were putting the finishing touches on their costumes and make-up. One of them beckoned to me, wiggling the crook of her finger. I started towards her when I felt an iron grip on the back of my shirt. It belonged to the bouncer. "Where do you think you're going, punk."

"He's OK, Jumbo. He's with it. He's Barry Kahn's kid. You know the flattie who works with Thousand Face Foxy?" The enforcer, who definitely earned his nickname, released his grip on me and said, "If ya' wanna come in here ya' gotta ask me first."

"Yessir, Mr. Jumbo. I will definitely talk to you first. I will never come in here again without checking with you." I slowly moved away from him. The woman who wiggled her finger at me did it again and I approached her.

I had never been in the presence of a grown woman in such suggestive circumstances. I could feel beads of sweat forming on my forehead and my heart was beating wildly.

She was wearing nothing but underwear as she prepared to put on her costume. She was pretty, in a dime-store kind of way. This was my initial experience of actually seeing a real woman up close with nothing on but bra and panties, and it made me very nervous. I had seen pictures in magazines, of course, but this was different. Way different. Her feminine aroma engulfed me. I felt flushed as blood rushed to my head. "So, you're Barry's kid, huh? I seen you on the carnival lot. You like the ladies, I see. Just like your old man. I'm Lily, what's your name?"

"K, Ke, Kenny," I stammered.

She looked me up and down and pronounced, "You're pretty cute. You ever been with a woman?" My physical state was a wreck by now. I was perspiring and suddenly had a raging hard-on. There was nowhere to look without seeing some part of her exposed skin, which did not help matters at all. "This is as close as I've ever been," I confessed.

She ran her fingers lightly up and down my body, giving my hard-on a direct squeeze which sent shock waves through my body. She looked directly into my eyes and said, "You're pretty young. Let me know when you're ready. For you, the first one is free."

She stood up, took my arm and guided me to a corner of the tent. "You can see everything from here. Nobody can see you. Watch me when I do my show. I'll give you a secret wink." Then she scurried off to don her costume.

The music blared the introduction of the dancing girls. One by one, they paraded across the stage. Each had a harem costume that had apparently been purchased from a Halloween store. The men crowded around the stage straining to get a better look. As each girl reached the end of the runway, she stopped in front of the panting crowd, did a suggestive set of wiggles and sexual moves, then removed a piece of her costume and slinked off back towards the entrance. The guys were whooping it up, stomping and yelling out crude remarks as each girl passed.

After the girls had made two passes in front of the audience, removing just enough clothing to inflame the imagination, they strutted off stage. The barker jumped up onto the stage and said, "Let's have a big round of applause for all of our lovely harem girls." The men whistled and clapped enthusiastically, demanding "More," and "Take it off."

The barker picked up on the cries. "Ya' say ya' want more? Well that's exactly what you're going to get. Behind this second curtain, the girls will reappear and give you what you want. There will be a separate admission of five dollars for this very special show. Step right up for the thrill of a lifetime!"

Most of the men shuffled out the exit, leaving a handful of others who were lining up to pay the extra money. Following a drum roll, Fatima wriggled across the stage accompanied by two of the harem girls, one of whom was my new friend, Lily, who was carrying a snake. Fatima faced the crowd and began a sensual dance. Then Lily approached her, and with the help of the other girl draped the snake around her neck. The star of the show then commenced to perform a simulated sex act with the reptile.

She allowed it to slither between her breasts then continue southward. She laid flat out on the stage and guided the snake between her legs. The two harem girls danced suggestively, on either side of her, running their hands over the length of their bodies. My eyes were bulging out of my head about two inches. At that point, Lily looked in my direction and gave me a sexy look.

After about ten minutes the show was over and the guys began filing out of the tent. "Didn't get to see her tits but for about 30 seconds," one guy muttered. "Aw, it's just another carnival scam," said another. No one seemed very satisfied.

Except me. I had just had the time of my young life. The visions of what I had just seen swirled around in my head. As I emerged into the daylight and fresh air, I was barely aware of my surroundings. I was in overwhelm. Nothing in my experience had prepared me for such an intimate encounter. I was still only vaguely aware of how love-making occurred, but my consciousness was pure sex, nonetheless. Life would never be the same again.

Freshman Year

When the summer ended, it was time for school to resume. I dreaded our homecoming to the stinking projects. For three months, I had been able to forget our living situation. Driving up to 1342 Crusado Lane brought it all back in a flash. The houseful of junkies, the ominous gang presence, and our financial destitution. They all awaited me with an unwavering sameness. Nothing had changed.

I noticed, however, that I had changed. The projects were no longer a mystery. I knew the scene. I had alternate routes that would allow me to successfully walk to the market, to school, and to the taco stand without getting beat-up or being robbed of my purchases. I had learned by now to obey my instincts for survival.

I kept to myself at school. I had not yet figured out where I fit in. As far as I could tell, the answer was, nowhere. I had made an irrevocable decision to prepare myself for college, so I enrolled in all college prep courses and focused my attention on my studies. I lived my life in a bubble, spending as much time as possible in the school library.

After school, I spent my afternoons on the football field. I joined the team out of a desire to have a good reason not to go home. I loved football, but there was not much glory being an interior offensive lineman on the sixth-string of the 'B' team. My teammates were almost all Mexican except for a few black guys. I'm pretty sure there was no racial tension. I noticed that Mexican guys had a tendency to mature physically at an early age. As a result, the school had an excellent 'B' team but not a very good varsity. We had a great year, going undefeated and winning the league title.

I got very little playing time. Only when the outcome of the game was assured did the coach empty the bench. My one moment of glory came in the last game of the season. We were in the last seconds of a victory against Marshall High School and had a sizeable lead when the coach called out, "Anyone who hasn't been in raise your hand." My hand shot into the air. There were no others. Coach reluctantly said, "OK, Kahn. Go in at linebacker."

Time was running out and it was probably the last play of the game. The last play of the season for that matter. It was obvious the opposition would try a desperation long pass. As the play unfolded, their quarterback rolled out to my side of the field. As he reared back to throw the ball, one of our linemen hit his arm causing the ball to wobble out of his hand and drift directly at me. I stood paralyzed as the fluttering ball headed straight at me.

When the ball was inches from my face, I put my hands up to protect myself from getting hit. The ball floated into my outstretched fingers and stuck there. I had INTER-CEPTED THE BALL! As I looked at it with great surprise, my teammates began screaming at me, "RUN! Run with the fuckin' ball!" I then realized that I could actually advance the ball if I moved my feet. I took two strides towards the goal when someone jumped me and dragged me to the ground. The gun went off. The game was over!

My sixth-string teammates piled on, then lifted me onto their shoulders and carried me off the field, as though I had just saved the day in the biggest game of the year. They triumphantly and noisily carried me all the way to the waiting school bus. The driver said, "You must have scored the winning touchdown." I looked at my sixth-string buddies and said, "I owe it all to my teammates." They burst into spontaneous agreement as though everyone knew WE would be the first-stringers next year.

Although the interception was a meaningless incident in a season where all I did was collect splinters from sitting on the bench, it provided me with a whole new set of fantasies. At night, after we turned out the lights, I imagined myself on some playing field with thousands of fans cheering me on as I swerved downfield, deftly dodging would-be tacklers to score the winning touchdown in the Rose Bowl game.

Home Sweet Home

36

As the sunny L.A. fall grayed into a rainy winter, things went from bad to worse in the house. All the money earned during the carnival season, which is supposed to get you through the winter, as any good carny will tell you, was gone. It disappeared into the glory holes in Mommy and Daddy's arms. Soon we were destitute again.

Once again, their heroin addictions took over with a vengeance. It became a mad obsession day and night. I would be awakened at 3:00 a.m. by the sound of screaming voices. Bitter, angry epithets, hurled at each other like small hand-grenades. It was always about dope, who got the most, and how much was left for the morning fix. Then it escalated into name-calling. "How could you use the last hit? You promised to save me some. You're a pig. A selfish pig."

"How about you? I left you a personal stash and you inhaled it immediately. You never thought about saving something then."

The arguments would go on throughout the night, escalating as the hours passed. By 5:00 a.m. they were reaching back to fight over issues from ten years ago. It was a non-stop brawl that kept me from getting any sleep. By the time they fell into bed, exhausted from the battle, it was time for me to get up. That was the exact time the baby would start crying. I was not only sleep-deprived, but my eardrums were taking a terrible beating.

I began snoozing in class. It was not difficult to get away with this though because nearly everyone in class was goofing off, drawing pictures, whispering to neighbors, shooting rubber bands, or taking a nap. It made me fit right in.

It was when I was fully awake, paying attention and asking probing questions that I didn't fit in. I found that I could get the rest I needed by just sinking into the mediocrity of the class.

My life had divided neatly into two halves. The terror of the house versus the sanity of the school. My head was

143

torn as well.

I wished I had someone I could confide in. But there was no one who would or could understand. I went over the various scenarios that might occur hundreds of times. I considered teachers, counselors or administrators at school. They could not even imagine LIFE in the projects much less junkie parents. I thought about involving other students but they had no idea of my circumstances, nor could they do anything about it if they did.

Blocks, Knives and Gold Leaf

As Christmastime rolled around, Barry roused himself from his drugged-out lifestyle to run some holiday scams. He and his buddy, Blackie Stein, drove to the wholesale district in downtown L.A. where they scored imitation expensive watches, or "blocks" as they were known, and sets of fake fine cutlery. The watches were cheap knock-offs, but looked like real Rolexes and other high-priced timepieces. The cheesy but attractive cutlery sets were impressively stamped with the mark of fine English silverwork. The items looked real to the untrained eye and made excellent Christmas gifts.

Barry and Blackie stashed the merchandise in the trunk of Barry's shitbox and then cruised the city looking for unsuspecting marks. Their favorite targets were gas stations where they could throw open the deck lid and display their wares. They did a landmark business. People jumped at the chance to acquire a genuine Rolex for two hundred dollars or a high-class knife set boxed in a red holiday-wrapped package for $20.

At the same time, their friend, No-Sox Bob, another out-of work carnie, introduced Dad to the gold sign business. This was the old and revered art of window and door printing known as "gold leaf," referring to block letter signs made with real gold. The application of the lettering is usually performed by a small group of artisans who have received years of training wherein they learn to expertly apply the letters made of the precious metal.

The carny hucksters knew little about the intricacies of gold leaf lettering, but they knew how to spray a window decal with gold paint. Unless you knew something about the technique, it was impossible to distinguish the real from the phony.

No-Sox Bob and Dad selected businesses at random to solicit. Barbershops were a prime target. But other businesses were hit as well; dry cleaners, furniture stores, accounting

145

offices, almost anyone who ran an establishment with a sign facing the street. Even small banks and insurance offices that already had real gold seal signs which were peeling or cracking were likely customers.

They brought me along to teach me how to first sell and then apply the letters. It was relatively simple, which was good because I was basically useless with my hands. I had never completed a single project in any shop class I had taken in school without the aid of more accomplished students. I ultimately achieved a minimal amount of skill with the letters which allowed me to perform passably well.

Business owners were duly impressed with the brochures we handed them. The pamphlets, which had been lifted from a respected, legit gold lettering company, then reproduced with our name on it, were complete with photos of prior jobs and enthusiastic quotes from satisfied customers. They were a great selling tool.

Most of our customers were impressed by the huge savings they would earn by using the services of "off-duty, professionally trained artisans" who were just seeking to make a few extra dollars for Christmas. We offered a lifetime warranty against cracking and peeling. Just call us anytime and we will be happy to come out and touch up your sign. Guaranteed. No questions asked.

The perfect lettering lasted about a week before cracks began to show. The business owners discovered that they had been taken about the same time the owners of the watches observed that they would not keep accurate time and the knife sets began to turn green.

It never ceased to amaze me how gullible people were. Did they really believe they were buying genuine Rolex watches from the trunk of a junky old car in a gas station? How could smart, successful business owners think they were purchasing real gold leaf lettering at a tiny fraction of its real worth? Did they stop to consider what they were getting or were they just brain-dead, or motivated by unvarnished greed? It remained a mystery to me. As P.T. Barnum said, "There's a sucker born every minute."

A Cry for Help

By mid-February, the holiday money was gone and Dad was dead in the water once again. The only cash I ever saw was the money I earned from mowing lawns or making deliveries for the butcher. Because I was so careful with my money, I always had a private stash which I could use if needed. I hoarded my savings like a miserly old penny-pincher. The coins accumulated and I relished adding to my treasure. I counted the dollars and coins every day. I had no particular plans for the cash, but just being able to look at it gave me a certain satisfaction.

Unfortunately, I was the only one in the house with spare cash. As a family, we had hit rock bottom. Rent and utility bills went unpaid. There was enough food for each meal, but nothing left over and an ever-increasing debt at Abe's market. Abe, accordingly, increased his demands regarding buying my baby sister. If he cut us off, there was no way to put anything on the table. A sense of desperation filled my days and nights. Where would we go if the county threw us out? Only the street was left.

On my own, I searched the city for some form of charity relief. My study led me to a Jewish agency apparently established to help Jewish families in need. I called and made an appointment for Mom and me to go apply for assistance. Late one afternoon, after school, she and I entered the building housing the agency.

The office looked like a typical bureaucracy with people working at wooden desks, typing, or talking on the telephone. We stood around for a while in the waiting area, waiting for the appointment to begin. Nobody came forward. Everyone was busy working on some invisible project. Eventually, we found someone who was willing to talk to us, an elderly lady with her hair in a tight bun. She motioned us to sit in front of her desk on two hard metal chairs.

"So, what do you want?" she asked in a flat tone. She

147

fiddled with some papers lying on the desk in front of her, giving the impression of being overwhelmed with work. Mom said, "We're a Jewish family living in public housing and have nothing to live on."

The lady looked up from her papers for a moment to give us the once over. "You look OK to me," she said. "What's the problem?"

Mom answered, "There are five of us including a baby. Our rent is unpaid, the utilities are about to be shut off, and we are barely able to get food on credit from the grocer where we already have a sizable overdue bill."

The lady scrunched her face in an expression of distaste and said, "Well, you seem to have managed to get along this far without charity, why do you need help now?"

Mom was beginning to get irritated. I could see she was on the edge of losing it. She hadn't wanted to come in the first place. I had to coax her into it. It was with the greatest reluctance that she eventually agreed.

"I just explained it to you," she said stiffly. "We're desperate. We're Jewish and we need a helping hand. That's why we came to your agency. That IS why you're here, isn't it?" The lady regarded us with disdain and said, "I'll give you an application to fill out." She handed Mom a sheaf of papers and directed her to a corner of the room to complete them.

The extent of the forms was daunting. They wanted to know every detail of our financial lives. How much money we earned, our bank accounts and employment information. Even though there were so many forms, it didn't take long to complete since all the answers were 'zero' or 'None.' Mom returned the completed forms to the lady, who scanned them carefully then said, "I have to show these to my manager."

She was gone for some time while we sat at her desk. When she returned she said, "We have reviewed your application and find that we cannot help you at this time." Mom looked at her questioningly. "Why not?" The lady shifted uncomfortably in her chair and said, "You're just too needy. We're not equipped to deal with the enormity of your problems."

Mom was getting exasperated. "But that's why we're here. Our whole family could be thrown out onto the street next

148

month." The agency woman retorted, "Your financial problems are simply beyond our limited means to help. You'll have to deal with it yourself."

We sat in stunned silence. The woman said, "You'll have to excuse me, now. I have work to do. Good bye and good luck." She lowered her head and began again to shuffle the papers on her desk.

Mom stood up, cupped her hands around her mouth and yelled out for all to hear, "No wonder people hate you fuckin' Jews. You can all die in hell. And the sooner, the better."

Everyone in the sprawling office stopped what they were doing and looked up at the madwoman spewing anti-Semitic curses. Mom stood at attention and continued. "What the hell are you looking at? You're no better than a collection of hogs with your snouts stuck in the ass of the Jewish community. Fuck you all." She grabbed my hand, spun me around and headed for the door.

She turned one last time before exiting to fire off a parting shot, "And fuck your families too."

That was our first, and only, attempt to find assistance in the Jewish community. Mom was furious for days. I had never seen her so angry. All she could talk about was "Those fuckin' fat-assed, big-nosed kikes" apparently overlooking the fact that we ourselves were part of that group. She held me directly responsible for the whole fiasco.

I made no further helpful suggestions.

Get Away Money

After the Jewish Agency disaster, I stayed away from our house more than ever. My usual retreat was the apartment across the courtyard occupied by the Delgado clan. The Delgado house never smelled too good. They were not terribly interested in domestic hygiene. I never saw them clean anything. There were always babies around shitting or throwing up all over the place.

It wasn't all that pleasant, but it was better than Horseface and Carlitos nodded out in our living room. Of my two choices, the Delgado apartment was the easy winner. A messy, smelly environment was vastly superior to Needle Central.

A new form of music called "rhythm and blues" was becoming vastly popular among teenagers. Musicians like Ray Charles, Fats Domino, and the Platters changed the social scene. Dancing was in. Luckily for me, there were plenty of female partners in the Delgado home to practice new steps with.

The advent of "doo wop" began with "Earth Angel," a sexy sound that encouraged the tight entwining of bodies. Soon we were experimenting both with swing moves and body-to-body grinding slow dancing. It was a fortunate development for me as I entered my teen years. Dancing was fun and rubbing up against busty pretty girls was even better.

As the winter warmed to spring, I was eager for Dad's carnival season to begin. It could not happen soon enough as far as I was concerned. The all-night screaming battles were escalating and taking a toll on me. Even the ear plugs which I purchased were of no use. The sound of their fights reverberated in my head even during the day when I was in school.

Everyone in our part of the projects knew what was happening. Our apartment was a notorious 'shooting gallery' with shabbily dressed addicts shuffling in and out at all hours. The Delgados were kind to never discuss the goings-on with me.

One day in spring, Dad had a chance to join a show that had some early season gigs. But he was so broke, he couldn't afford the gas to get there. There was no one he could borrow a dime from and it looked liked he would be stuck in the quicksand of his lifestyle. I overheard him and Mom lamenting the situation non-stop for two days. I kept hoping something would break. Getting him out of the house would be an immediate relief.

On day three, when I returned home from my after-school job with the butcher, my parents told me to sit down at the kitchen table. "We have something to discuss with you," Mom said. I was taken aback because they NEVER had anything to discuss with me. Dad looked uncomfortable and avoided eye contact with me, choosing instead to fiddle with the salt shaker.

Mom said, "Dad has a chance to get some work. He got a call from Thousand Face Foxy to join a show in northern California. He wants to go but he has no get-away money. I hate to ask, but I know you have some savings. You don't have to let us have it if you don't want to."

I had slightly over a hundred dollars hidden away. It had taken me forever to save it up. While I had no particular plans for my nest egg, I was keenly aware of how difficult it had been for me to accumulate it. I was in a difficult spot. That savings represented my hard-earned efforts to achieve a glimmer of independence. On the other hand, if I refused, the old man might not be able to go to work. I desperately wanted him out of the house.

Dad said, "You don't have to. But if you do, it's a loan. I'll repay when I get on my feet. I can make good money on the road."

I pushed my chair back, went to the small bedroom I shared with my little brother and retrieved a hundred dollars. I brought it back to the kitchen table where they were still seated and handed it to my father. They both let out a sigh of relief as I turned over my life savings. I knew I would never see it again. I felt empty and broke, but at least the madness of the raging scene in our home would end for awhile. It was worth it.

As soon as he left town, things improved. Life settled down to a regular, quiet routine. I was no longer afraid to come home. I was playing on the high school baseball team, which practiced every afternoon, but now it was more for fun than to avoid the scene in Ramona Gardens.

I still spent countless hours with the Delgados, dancing or feeling up Mary. I went back to looking for work, now that I was broke again. But even having empty pockets felt a lot better than dealing with the insanity of heroin addiction.

I guess everything in life is relative. If you are living in a madhouse, ordinary poverty looks pretty good.

Summer Vacation

Summer of '55 came as a great relief. Once again the entire family left the confines of the Ramona Gardens housing projects to hit the road. I was relieved on several levels. I was having a terrible time in school. Nobody would talk to me. I was an outcast, unable to fit in anywhere.

One time we had a school outing to see the inner workings of a newspaper, the *L.A. Times*. My homeroom teacher had us fill out a form which required us to select three students who we would like to sit next to on the school bus. I selected the names of the least popular kids in the class thinking I might find another outcast who would accept me. No such luck. Not one other kid was willing to sit next to me. I skipped the trip, preferring to sit by myself in the library.

Needless to say, leaving our stinking apartment to the roaches and escaping the junkies and gangs for three months was also greatly appreciated. I always tended to neglect the fact that we would have to return in the fall.

We spent that summer season in Oregon and Washington, two of the most beautiful states in the union. I had never seen such lush, green landscapes filled with roaring rivers, streams, waterfalls and hillsides black with thick, wooded forests and abundant wildlife. Of course, Dad would never stop to allow us to enjoy any of these natural wonders. To him, it was just a matter of getting from one fair to another as quickly as possible.

Each journey was an opportunity for Dad to educate us on the ways of the world. One of his favorite subjects was "who to trust." He lectured us at length. "Don't trust anybody in this world except your own family. Nobody. Everyone will take advantage of you, if you give 'em a chance. It doesn't matter if it's a girlfriend or a buddy. Don't ever think you have a friend because you don't. People are only out for one thing, and that is to get what they can from you. If they pretend that they like you, it's only to put you off guard."

Then, warming to the subject, he continued, "You're ahead of the game if you KNOW people are going to take advantage of you at every opportunity. Your job in life is to get them first. Don't ever trust anyone outside the family because they have only one thing in mind: separating you from your dough. Whatever they say, you have to remember there are no friends in this world. Whoever you meet is only looking out for Number One. Number One is the beginning and end of every human contact. Trust no one. *Ever!*"

He drilled the lesson home with a thousand examples. "Carnies are the lowest form of life. They'll steal a crust of bread from a starving man. They have no conscience. I've seen these thieves steal anything that wasn't nailed down. And if it IS nailed down, they'll lie down next to it and swear it's theirs."

His pervasive distrust encompassed every phase of our lives. We were instructed NEVER to answer a knock at the door. We were told to get either Mom or Dad to do it. No friends were permitted inside the house, ever. In addition, we were forbidden to spend an overnight at any friend's house, which was not a big problem for me since I had no friends.

In 1955, I was now 14 years old. I was becoming increasingly aware of a number of changes in my body. My voice was deepening, I was growing hair in places that used to be baby smooth and my interest in girls had skyrocketed. I began to see the opposite sex as an object of great desire, a development which subsequently overwhelmed my entire life.

Whereas I had previously regarded females as a somewhat pleasant, although useless, part of the background, they were rapidly becoming a highly sought-after object of my desire. While I still had only the vaguest idea of the mechanics of sex, the feminine dynamic slowly but surely occupied an increasing segment of my waking hours. I knew little about girls, but I definitely wanted one.

There were lots of them on the carnival grounds. Many were of little or no interest because they were too old or too young. Girls with families or boyfriends were also excluded. Still, there was a fair share in the right age group wandering about the midway. I studied the techniques of the older guys to see how they managed the situation.

No-Sox Bob was my mentor. At age 26, he had been scouting the female scene for a number of years. He pointed out pretty young mark girls who gave off signs of being available. He taught me how the ones out alone were better than those in groups. They were easier to talk to. He showed me how to get their attention. "Chicks dig plush," he said. "I've scored with a purple poodle more times than I can count. Some of 'em will do ANYTHING for a stuffed animal. Once they get their heart set on a cuddly prize, you've got 'em."

I was unsure what "scoring" actually meant, but it sounded good. Girls were like creatures from another planet and I wanted to see what made them tick, up close. I was determined to find one I could be alone with to continue my exploration. I didn't know how to get started but, luckily, Bob was willing to share his knowledge.

"We have an ideal position," he explained. "We are able to see large numbers of potential partners just because we're out here all day. Since these chicks have basically boring lives, the carnival is exciting to them. The County Fair is a big deal that happens once a year, like Christmas. And we can make it even more exciting by giving them a chance to glimpse an inside look at our fascinating lives." He laughed at his irony because he was well aware of the countless boring hours we stood around doing nothing.

"Don't tell them you're from L.A. Say you live in Hollywood and run into movie stars all the time. They love that crap." He also taught me to use the thrill rides as an attraction. Since I was "with it," I could take a girl on any of the rides for free, and, as a special bonus, not have to wait in line. Lastly, and perhaps most importantly, I could hold out the hope that she could wind up with that adorable purple poodle she longed for so badly if she played her cards right.

The approach worked incredibly well. Since I was in the business of persuading people to play my game, I talked to almost everyone who passed in front of the joint all day long. When a single, cute young girl showed up, I knew just what to do. I first pretended that she was just another customer and all I wanted was to get her to play the game. Once I had her attention, the rest was easy.

We were in Medford, Oregon when I first gave it a try. I was working the "punk rack" at the time. It was a game that required the player to throw balls at rows of small, furry objects lined up on the shelves. They were painted to look like small cats with long whiskers. There was no "G" or "Gaff" on the joint. I could not control who might win or lose. A lucky mark could hit three cats and win a plush prize.

But it was a lot more difficult than it looked. The cats appeared to be larger targets than they actually were due to their construction. Most of each cat's exterior outline was just thick fur covering the body that would allow the ball to pass right through without disturbing the cat at all. It took a very lucky shot to hit a cat directly, so we lost very few prizes.

On a late Tuesday afternoon things were very slow. Only a few stragglers wandered up and down the midway. Then I saw her. She was about my age, very cute, and had her yellow hair in pigtails which absolutely knocked me out. The girls at Lincoln High School definitely did not wear their hair in pigtails. It was a country thing and it entranced me. She wore a pink dress with matching pink lipstick. My heart began to flutter.

I was casually tossing a ball from one hand to another when she passed. I called out to her, "Knock down three cats and win the prize of your choice." She glanced at me and shrugged, "I don't think so. I'm not a very good ballplayer." I knew she wouldn't play the game, but that was fine. I really didn't want her to. "In that case," I said, "You can have a free game on the house." She stopped for a moment and gave the joint the once-over. "I would like to have one of those neat stuffed poodles."

Bells began going off in my head. It was clearly the right sign according to No-Sox. I held out a ball to her. "Go ahead, give it a try. You have nothing to lose." She looked at me questioningly. "You mean it? I can play for free?"

"Absolutely," I answered handing her the ball. What I meant to say was, "You can have anything you want, including my entire earnings for the week."

She took the ball from me and set herself to throw it. The ball missed everything. I gave her another with the same result. "I guess you're right," I said. "Maybe pitching is not your thing." I hesitated a moment then added, "You should stick to the rides." She smiled and replied, "I think you're right." She turned to leave and I jumped over the counter to join her. "I'm taking a break right now. If you'd like to check out the Ferris wheel, I'd be happy to join you. My treat."

She stopped momentarily to consider the proposal. "OK," she said, "Sounds like fun." As we strolled down the midway, I felt like I had just won the lottery. I received nods of approval and winks from the other carnies as we passed each joint.

I eventually took her on every ride, ignoring the fact that I had a job waiting for me. Job, shmob, who gave a damn. I was with this beautiful angel and would gladly have suffered a dismissal from my position. That is, if I had thought about it, which I didn't.

As the afternoon faded into evening, we wandered into the food court of the fair and had dinner. I was proud to have plenty of spare money in my pocket. I felt like a big shot. It was a great feeling. We talked about her life and mine.

"So what's life like on a farm?" I asked. "Lots of hard work," she answered. "We get up early and go until night. There are so many chores to do, we never seem to finish. I begin at daybreak and work for three hours before going to school. Then I have more tasks when I get home. How about you? What's your life like? It must be exciting traveling with the carnival."

"We work long hours, too. Even though we don't open until eleven in the morning, closing time is midnight. The work is harder than it looks. But there are rewards as well. Like meeting you, for instance." She blushed. I continued, "Of course, this is only a summer job. I go back to school in the fall. School is OK, but we don't have any girls as pretty as you."

"What school do you go to?" she asked. "Hollywood High School," I lied, hoping to impress her. It did. "Wow. Do you ever see any movie stars like Clark Gable or Marilyn Monroe?"

"Oh sure. James Dean and Sal Mineo shop where we do. And sometimes I see John Wayne at the gas station. I've only seen Marilyn a few times. She doesn't go out much."

By the time dinner was over, she was thoroughly impressed. "Oh wow, look at the time," she said. "I have to be in by nine. I'd better get going." I accompanied her to the front gate. "I'll walk part way with you," I offered. "Oh, thanks. But don't you have to get back to work?"

I had totally forgotten about my job. It didn't seem very important at the moment. "Not really. My dad owns the carnival. I come and go as I please." We walked hand-in-hand down the road leading from the fairgrounds.

The further we got from the noisy carnival the better I felt. The clatter of the rides and barking carnies gave way to crickets and clear night air. I felt transported to some paradise, an untouched Garden of Eden where all was peaceful and calm. It was a perfect moment.

We stopped, kissed, then we did it again. A million zillion stars sparkled in the heavens. I wanted this to last forever.

Of course it didn't. When we got to a certain corner she said, "I have to go alone from here. If you like, I can come back to the fair tomorrow."

"I'd like that a lot," I responded enthusiastically. With a warm, farewell kiss we parted.

I was on cloud nine until I returned to the midway. My boss was standing in the joint, furious. I was working for 'Red' Holiday, also known on the carnival lot as N.G. Red, or simply N.G. The N.G. stood for No Good. No one called him that to his face, but it was well understood that he deserved the nickname.

He went ballistic when he saw me. "You worthless punk," he spat out. "You left the joint during the hottest part of the night. We couldn't handle the play. Where were you, you little shit? Out chasing gash like your old man?"

I was floored by the intensity of his anger. I knew what I had done was unforgivable. I had cost the boss money. That was the biggest sin of all. And I had no good excuse. "Turn in your apron," he demanded. "You're fired."

I handed him the apron. He counted the money and gave me my cut. I turned and walked off, thoroughly embarrassed. I worried about what I would say to my father. Dad would definitely not take this well. And I didn't know if I could get another job. I had visions of being sent back to the projects to spend the summer in our crummy apartment alone. A black cloud enveloped me. It was the low point of my carny career.

Luckily, Dad squashed the beef with some drugs, and I returned the next day. I'd learned a valuable lesson I wouldn't soon forget. Keep your dick out of the cash register.

Tenth Grade

The fall of 1955 began my second year in the projects. In a strange way, I had become accustomed to my surroundings. There was a familiarity to it all. Humans must be the most incredibly adaptable creatures of all. The disgusting neighborhood with its ever-present gang activity, our crummy apartment filled with low-life junkies, and even the roaches seemed like no big deal now. I knew what to expect and how to survive both physically and psychologically.

I had discovered alternate routes to everywhere I had to go; school, the market and after school jobs. The art of invisibility was my guiding principle. I had no real friends but I knew everyone's name. I could roam nearly every street and alley in Ramona Gardens in my sleep. I could almost tell you who lived in each apartment, where the turf divided between the black and the Mexican gangs and what time they congregated.

School was the only place I felt completely safe. I loved Abraham Lincoln High School. As a physical structure, it was as beautiful as a school could be. One of the original seven high schools in Los Angeles, it had first been built in 1913, on a hillside overlooking North Broadway. An earthquake demolished the school, and it was rebuilt on the flatlands below in 1929, leaving only the gymnasium and playing fields on the original site. A bridge connected the two. Great stretches of green grass accented the fine, traditional buildings.

The school was my safe haven. Whatever activities students engaged in outside the school grounds, they were on their best behavior inside the confines of Lincoln. Even the worst of the bad dudes didn't last long, either dropping out or transferring. I never recalled having a threatening experience on campus.

The classes were generally full but not overcrowded. While there was plenty of horseplay, it never got so disruptive that it interfered with instruction if you wanted it. If I could choose to live there full time, I would have jumped at the chance.

158

It was life outside the protective school walls that constituted the real challenge for me. After classes, I trekked across
the bridge to the playing fields on the hillside next to the
main school. This was my second year on the 'B' football
team and I was slotted to be a starter. That meant a lot to me.
The long hours of practice under the broiling September sun
gave me a physical outlet for my inner aggression. I didn't
know it at the time, but the heavy hitting probably saved my
life. At least my inner life.

Although I seldom acknowledged it, I was longing to lash
out at someone or something. I kept myself so busy that there
was little time to sort out how I felt about things. I was
trapped in the projects and there was no way out. My parents barely knew I was alive and certainly never asked me
any questions. I was well aware that nobody gave a damn
about my well-being.

I kept wishing there was at least one person who I could
confide in. Someone to talk to about my situation. But there
was no such person. Even if there had been, I would not have
had the nerve to communicate the full extent of my parents'
heroin addiction. I was terrified the information would be
passed on to the authorities, who would then demolish my
family, send Mom and Dad to jail and my brother and sister
and me to foster families again, or worse, to county holding
facilities such as Maclaren Hall, a nightmare institution for
abandoned children.

Smashing my body into tackling dummies or other players provided a much-needed outlet. The physical contact
drained much of my pent-up frustration and left me happily
exhausted at the end of each school day.

My coaches were thrilled to see such unbridled aggression and rewarded it with a starting spot at offensive right-
guard. My new found status elevated my spirit and boosted
my self-esteem. I was proud of being in a starting position
on the team and walked around campus with my head held
high. Unknown to me, the other kids saw it as just another
sign of snobbishness and avoided me in droves.

I didn't much care since I was the one who trotted onto
the field at the start of each game and reveled in the faint
applause from the handful of students scattered throughout

the grandstand. To me, it was the equivalent of running onto the field at the Rose Bowl with the U.C.L.A. Bruins to the cheers of tens of thousands of screaming fans. I couldn't have been happier.

We had a great year and won the league championship largely due to the heroics of two elusive scatbacks, a pint-sized scooter named Tommy Huitron and his partner, my friend A.J. from the projects. Neither one was very big, but both had great moves and an athlete's heart. I was satisfied to lay blocks that sprang them into the open field. They got the cheers but that didn't matter to me. I knew they couldn't have had such success moving the ball forward without the unsung efforts of grunts like me in the front line.

When the football season ended, I tried out for the baseball team. The skills I had acquired on the playing fields at Rancho Park enabled me to make the team. I wasn't very good but I loved to play the game. I was a decent catcher, but my weak throwing arm made it nearly impossible to make the peg from home plate to second base. I could hit fairly well to the opposite field mostly because I had trouble getting the bat around on the pitch. But it looked like I knew what I was doing. Most importantly, I was able to avoid going back to the hated projects for a few more hours each day.

I had dreams of having a great career on the gridiron or the baseball diamond but I knew they were just dreams because of my limited ability. Nevertheless, the dreams were important to me.

A Holiday Surprise

As December rolled around, I dreaded having to leave the protective confines of Lincoln High School for the two whole weeks of Christmas vacation. After classes on the last Friday before the break, I dawdled on the two-mile walk from school to Ramona Gardens. The longer it took to get home, the better. There was no baseball practice that day so I had no excuse to stay away.

When I arrived, I was greeted by a sight that I could not fully comprehend. Our living room was filled with stunning, well-dressed college girls, instead of the usual smelly, nodded-out junkies. Every spare inch of the apartment was piled high with decorated gift boxes. Mom was flitting about with an enthusiasm I had seldom encountered.

She ran up to me and stated, "Honey, these angels have come to make our holidays truly wonderful." One of the girls approached me and gave me a hug as the others gathered around. "My name is Rebecca," she said. "We all belong to a Jewish sorority at the University of Southern California, and I'm the house president. Our project this Hanukah was to gather gifts for Jewish families on welfare."

I was in awe. So many beauties in our pathetic home was more than I could take. My first thought was that I hoped no roaches showed up. "Y, You certainly are generous," I stammered. "I've never seen so many gifts in my life."

The girls giggled. One of them said, "Tell him the whole story, Rebecca." The president explained, "We worked as hard as we could to accumulate as many presents as possible for the past six weeks. We held bake sales and conducted raffles every weekend. We hit up our parents and relatives and anyone else who was willing to contribute." Another girl chimed in, "And don't forget the donations from the deli owners."

She pointed to a pile of boxes from which were emanating delicious aromas. "The people we asked to contribute were most generous. But then we had an unforeseen problem. We couldn't find any Jews on welfare." All the girls laughed at the same time, nodding their heads in agreement.

161

"We hadn't thought to check to see who we were going to give all this stuff to. We simply assumed that there was a list of needy families."

Rebecca continued, "We formed a committee to investigate the situation. After a thorough search, we discovered only one family. Yours." All the girls applauded. Another said, "Thank God we found you. I don't know what we would have done with all this stuff otherwise."

By this time my head was spinning. I wasn't sure if I was more astounded with the huge supply of presents, the gorgeous well-dressed college girls, or the fact that we were the only Jewish family on welfare. It was as though the Martians had decided to land in our living room, bearing gifts from another planet.

I was now getting nervous that a couple of the local junkies would stop by for a fix while they were there. I started to imagine what I would say. "Oh, girls I'd like to introduce you to Horseface Joe. He just stopped by to borrow a cup of heroin. He and Daddy are going upstairs to shoot up in the bathroom. They'll only be gone a minute. If you'd like to stick around a while, maybe we can get them to show you how to cut the smack with powdered sugar."

The Jewish girls from USC hung around for a couple of hours before returning to their sorority house, leaving me to dream of what college life must be like. I was more sure than ever that I was destined to find out. I had no clue that these students were all the privileged offspring of upscale families who could afford to shell out thousands and thousands of dollars per semester to keep their precious daughters living in the lap of luxury.

The presents they brought insured us the best holidays ever. The goodies lasted well into January.

Time Out

In the spring of 1956, I began getting signs from my body that all was not well. I started experiencing pains in my back. I often awakened in the middle of the night feeling extremely uncomfortable and could not get back to sleep. Each episode lasted only a few days but became progressively worse as time went on. I continued my school routine, including playing baseball in the afternoons, but my enthusiasm was dampened by sleepless nights. I presumed that the discomfort would pass and did my best to ignore it.

One day in school, the pain became unbearable and I excused myself from class to go to the nurse's office. She took my temperature and suggested I lie down on a cot for awhile. After half an hour, the pain did not subside and the nurse informed me that I was running a fever. She said, "If you want I'll call your parents and they can come pick you up."

I said OK. She called, but no one answered the phone at home. She tried several times but to no avail. The folks were probably somewhere getting loaded.

After a couple of hours during which the pain was becoming unbearable, the nurse asked, "Do you want to go to the hospital? There's nothing more I can do for you here." I said yeah. She said, "We have no way to transport you there. You'll have to get there on your own."

I knew exactly where L.A. County General Hospital was because it was not that far from the projects. I passed it nearly every day. It was a couple of miles from Lincoln. I got up from the cot, almost doubled over from the pain, but managed to stagger to the front of the school and out onto the street.

I got no more than ten or fifteen yards when I had to stop to rest and allow the pain to subside, then I continued on. In this manner I was able to reach the hospital in about three hours. By this time the pain was excruciating. My legs were shaky and my vision began to blur.

The entrance to the hospital consisted of about a hundred steps which I managed partly on my hands and knees. I eventually staggered in the front door and made my way

163

to the information desk. I was directed to an intake clerk where they took down some information, then ordered me to wait in a long line of patients waiting to see a doctor.

I had never before encountered such a mass of tortured humanity. People in the most grotesque conditions were writhing on gurneys which stretched as far as the eye could see. Old people with a family member standing by, young people with knife wounds bleeding profusely, and countless others with unknown maladies lay helplessly in the crowded corridors. Not a single doctor was in sight. I found an empty gurney near a broom closet, pushed it to the end of the line and clambered onto it. The sights and smells emanating from the hallway were beyond description.

There was nothing to do but wait. An elderly Mexican lady who was standing next to the person ahead of me approached and asked, "Is there anything I can do for you?" I shook my head, unable to speak. "Can I get you some water?" she inquired. My throat was parched and I realized that I had had nothing to drink in several hours. The severe pain deadened my recognition of my thirst. I nodded my head and she disappeared from my vision, returning in a couple of minutes with a small paper cup of water. I downed it and asked for another. She refilled it several times. I thought she must have been an angel.

I blacked out then. When I regained consciousness, I was being wheeled down another corridor by a black orderly dressed in hospital garb. He noticed my eyes flutter open and said, "Don't worry man, we're going to take good care of you now." I was so grateful, tears began to fill my eyes and I went out again.

He guided me into an examination room where I lay alone for some time. At some point, a doctor entered the room and said, "Well, young man, let's see what we have here. I'm going to run a few preliminary tests. Try to get as comfortable as you can." I begged him for something to relieve the pain in my back. "I can't give you anything yet," he explained. "First, we need to complete our tests. I imagine you're concerned about having polio."

POLIO!!! The word shot through me like a bullet from a high-powered gun. POLIO? I knew nothing of the disease except that it was horrible and victims were confined to iron lungs just to be able to breathe. A doctor Salk had recently discovered a compound that would inoculate people from the dreaded disease, but it had not reached the housing projects where I lived. It never crossed my mind that I might have contracted it. It was incomprehensible.

While these devastating thoughts engulfed me, the doctor returned and said, "We're going to do a spinal tap on you just to make sure. Do you know what that is?" I shook my head. I had never heard of it before. All I knew was that the pain was so intense, I began to scream.

"You have to calm down for us to be able to do the procedure. We're going to take some fluid from your spine." It sounded horrible to me. I gathered whatever strength I had left and forced myself not to cry. I said, "It sounds awful." He replied, "Well, it's not much fun and it's pretty painful, but it won't take much time."

They wheeled me into another room, took off my shirt and explained that they had to draw a bull's-eye on my back. They would then stick a needle into the center of the bull's-eye and extract some spinal fluid. It was a touchy procedure and didn't always work the first time, the doctor explained.

They placed me on a table, told me to sit up and grab my knees while they inserted the needle. I nearly went through the roof. Then it was over and I was allowed to lie down again. After about an hour, the doctor returned and said the procedure didn't work and they would have to do it again. I had no choice but to subject myself to the agony once again.

When the doctor returned after the second test he said, "It is polio. Non-paralytic. You're in the contagious stage right now. We're going to transfer you to the CDU, the Contagious Diseases Unit. You will remain there until this stage passes. I'm sorry but we can't give you anything for your pain right now. You'll just have to gut it out."

For the next three days, I endured the most agonizing, intense pain I had ever experienced in my entire life. Polio ran through my body just tearing it to shreds. The experience blurred into one long nightmare.

After the three days, the doctors came to me and explained that although the strain of polio I had contracted was non-paralytic, the disease had gone through my body and destroyed muscle tissue that would never come back. And, that I was going to be in the hospital for a long time.

Within a week, the contagious part of the disease was over and had effectively eliminated half the muscle tissue on the left side of my body. My left arm and left leg were so thin I could encircle them with the finger and thumb of one hand.

When my mother came to visit me, there was a thick glass partition between us and we had to speak over a telephone. There was not much to say, but I had never seen her so concerned about me. It was comforting. It made the pain a little more bearable.

White Memorial

At the end of my week in the contagious diseases unit of General Hospital, I was transferred to White Memorial Hospital in East L.A. I didn't know why that particular facility was selected, but it turned out to be the best possible institution for my particular medical condition. It was run by Seventh-Day Adventists, of whom I knew nothing, and had a strong connection to Loma Linda, a cutting edge research hospital with an extensive polio unit.

Installed in a two-person room, equipped with all the comforts of home, it was much better than MY home, with remote control TV, unlimited telephone privileges, and a bay window.

On my first day there, I was introduced to my managing physician, Dr. Youngberg, a lanky good-looking man with kind eyes. He was soft spoken but firm. "You're not getting out of bed. Period. You have an extensive recovery process ahead of you. The damage from the polio germ is finished. What remains is a long, difficult rehabilitation process."

I was taken aback. I had no idea of the true extent of my disability. "When will I be able to get up?" I asked. He stroked his clean-shaven, well-defined chin and said, "That's hard to say. We'll have to see how your body responds to the physical therapy we have planned for you."

As he examined my left leg he said, "Downstairs there is a complete set of recovery hardware including whirlpool baths, hot-towel tables, and exercise machines. You will also have physical therapists visiting you nearly every day to put you through a tough exercise regimen. For now, it is most important that you NOT get out of bed. If you need anything, just push the red button on the end of the cord next to your bed. That's about it for now. I'll be back to see you in a couple of days. Just relax and don't worry about a thing."

His manner was so reassuring that I knew I was in capable hands. He looked like he'd been hand-selected by central casting, with a gentle demeanor, soft eyes and a confident aura about him.

I had no problem complying with his orders. I was happy just to be out of pain. It was strange to examine my own limbs and see such a marked difference between my right side and left side. One looked perfectly normal and the other about half its size. But it didn't matter much at the moment since I had no tasks to perform with either one.

There was no one in the bed next to mine, but I was told that another patient was due in the next day. Several nurses took turns seeing to my needs. Each one reflected a sense of caring I had seldom encountered in my world. I felt like visiting royalty with every wish granted almost immediately. I was provided with a fistful of menus to fill out for meals for the entire week, a TV Guide, and information regarding a mobile library from which I could select reading materials. I felt like I was on vacation. At least, I imagined what a vacation might be, since I had never actually been on one.

The next day, I got my new roommate, a young black man, about 23 years old, who had the same type of polio I had contracted. His name was Eddie and he had been a professional boxer before he fell ill. His muscle tissue damage was not as widespread as mine, concentrated primarily in his lower left leg which had all but withered away. He had a big smile and was the hippest cat I ever met. He immediately accepted me even though we were separated by enough years to put us at distinctly different stages in life. He was a man and I still an emerging teenager. I had much to learn from him and he, generously, was a willing teacher.

Very soon I got my first lesson. The subject was sex. The instruction was more show-and-tell than lecture. He had a beautiful young girlfriend who came to visit in the late afternoon. He forewarned me that they were going to enclose his bed with the curtain surrounding it. I was requested to act as lookout in case any curious nurse happened to stick her nose in the door. I propped myself up on the foot of the bed where I could keep an eye on the door. His girl placed a chair in front of it so it would block the entrance should anyone accidentally push it.

I didn't see what they were doing but the sounds were pretty graphic. Luckily, we were visitor-free for the next forty-five minutes. When he opened the curtain, both of them were grinning from ear to ear. My education was just beginning. In the following weeks, I learned more about life than I had in ten years in school.

Hospital Life

My physical therapy began a few days later. An orderly came to my room, rolled me onto a gurney, and pushed me to the elevator where we descended into the basement where the heavy rehab equipment was located.

I was placed on a special bed where heavy, hot pads were laid on my body. They were very, very hot. I was encouraged not to resist the extreme temperature. They assured me that the process worked best at the highest degree I could stand. One heavy pad after another was piled onto my stretched out body until I couldn't move. They were left there until they began to cool, then replaced with a new steaming batch.

After the hot pads, I was dipped into a still hotter whirlpool bath while a technician gently rotated my limbs. Despite the discomfort, I was impressed by the amount of personalized attention I received.

The hot pad/whirlpool therapy constituted my daily morning routine. On my journey down the hallway back, I was able to see into other rooms. I was amazed to see other patients who were in much worse shape than I was. Many were confined to metallic casings known as "iron lungs." The orderly who transported me explained that those patients could not survive outside the confines of their support system.

Eventually, I persuaded him to roll me into some of the rooms so I could meet some of the trapped victims face-to-face. For the most part, they were an incredibly cheery group. I never heard a single complaint from any of the patients in all the months I was in the hospital. We discussed their families, their hobbies, and their lives before being confined to the hospital.

I felt lucky that I had not been afflicted with the paralytic form of polio. I didn't know if I would be as courageous as my newfound friends. They exuded a brand of spirituality I could not even imagine. Thanks to their attitude, I never experienced one moment of sadness at my own condition.

When I returned to my bed, I was served lunch, then prepared for an afternoon of strength training under the direction of a physical therapist who started the long process of building me back up as much as possible. The only way to achieve a return to an almost fully functional body was to redevelop the muscle tissue that was not destroyed by the disease. It was impossible to determine whether there was enough left to accomplish that goal. Only time would tell.

After a few weeks, I began feeling fine and ready to move on my own. I believed that the doctor's admonition to stay in bed was unnecessarily cautious. There was no question in my mind that I could make it to the bathroom under my own strength and avoid having to use the dreaded bed pan.

Waiting for the perfect moment, when my roommate was out for his therapy and there was no one else around, I sat up and dangled my legs over the edge of the bed, then lowered myself onto the cool floor for the first time since being hospitalized. I was wrong. I immediately collapsed in a heap, knocking over the tray holding the water pitcher, making a loud, clattering sound that reverberated throughout the entire floor.

I was more embarrassed than injured and tried to pull myself back onto the bed quickly to avoid a serious scolding. No such luck. I fell a second time, knocking over a potted plant as several nurses came rushing into the room. Water was everywhere and I was bleeding from both my knee and my elbow.

Doctor Youngberg was furious when he found out what happened. I had no idea he was capable of being so angry. Wrong again. He nearly had a stroke as he chewed me out for a solid half hour. I swore I would never again ignore his instructions. "You'd better not try that again," he warned. I knew he meant it.

I soon realized that my mind was able to see myself moving about freely, but my body was not on the same page. It was a lesson I would not forget.

The Good Life

I eventually discovered that White Memorial was a Seventh-Day Adventist hospital. I had no idea what this meant, but I quickly found out. My nurses were a dedicated band of people committed to the highest values. To them, caregiving was more than a job. They showed a type of concern that came from an elevated sense of service.

The women assigned to my well-being did more than simply see to my needs. They displayed a warmth and interest level that went well beyond the call of duty. They considered themselves Christians in the highest sense of the word. They gave from their hearts and expected nothing in return. It made a deep impression on me.

Several times they tried to get me to read the *Bible*, but I didn't see the connection between words written centuries ago by who knows who, and the daily sharing of real compassion. To me, their actions spoke louder than words. I respected them for their attitude and the manner in which they treated me. That spoke volumes.

They were also strictly vegetarian. I tried my best to adjust to veggie-burgers, but somehow it just wasn't the same as an old-fashioned beefy American hamburger. I asked Mom to smuggle me forbidden goodies when she came to visit, which she did quite regularly. She would pack up the baby, take my little brother by the hand, and make the trek to the hospital. In a strange way, I felt that she took notice of me for the first time in my life.

Since I had unlimited phone privileges, we spoke every night for hours. Both of us tuned our radios onto the same rhythm and blues station and listened to the new brand of music while we rapped. Our favorite DJ was Huggie Boy, an emerging star on the radio dial.

We loved the doo-wop sound. The Drifters, the Platters and Clyde McPhatter were our favorites. She never spoke of my condition and, as a result, I didn't think of it at all.

I was quite comfortable in my new surroundings. Everything was clean and well-ordered, unlike the gritty housing projects I had gotten used to but still despised.

First LOVE

As spring turned to summer in 1956, I had an incredible event occur in my confined hospital life. I received a phone call from a young girl who had heard of my situation. Her name was Bobbi Maizel, a 13-year old who lived in the Jewish Fairfax district. She sounded great on the phone and we soon communicated for hours every day.

Each call brought us closer even though we had never met or seen one another. Her phone calls rapidly became the center of my existence. We found much to talk about even though our lives were strikingly different. Countless hours spent on the telephone soon turned to a deep emotional attachment. At least on my part.

After a few weeks, I asked her if she would consider visiting me. It was a bold request considering she had no way to get from West L.A. to East L.A. other than public transportation, which was always miserable in our city. Municipal buses were painfully slow, required several transfers and ran infrequently. In addition, they were really no place for a proper young lady from a good Jewish family. She politely declined my request, pointing out the time-consuming hardships involved. I understood, but continued to press the issue until she finally agreed.

She had considerable difficulty getting her parents' approval. Eventually, they relented and a date was set for her initial visit. On a Saturday afternoon, she showed up at my bedside.

I was stunned. She was the most beautiful creature I had ever laid eyes on. For the first time in my life I was speechless. If I thought I was in love with Bobbi before I met her, it was nothing compared to how I felt after seeing her in person. She was beyond my fondest imaginings. She was an angel. The answer to my dreams. There was a God, after all.

I thought my heart would burst from my chest. The sight of her made my eyes happy. She was a budding girl-woman, an exquisite blend of the innocence of youth and the feminine soul of the ages. I could not have fallen harder if I had been pushed off the roof of the hospital where I occasionally basked in the summer sun. All I asked of life was to be eternally in her presence. The touch of her hand was like heaven. A beautiful place that I'd never known in my short life.

The hours went by all too quickly. When she kissed me good-bye, I felt a happiness of a new and unique type. I had a silly grin that would not go away, no matter what. Life was good.

In the ensuing weeks and months, she became the molten center of my universe. When we spoke on the phone, our conversations had a whole new depth. I had an image to attach to the voice. And what an image it was. There was no doubt that I was the luckiest person on the face of the globe. I glowed in the aura of our newfound mutual affection. For the first time I believed that Love was real, and not just the motivation for so many popular songs. It existed in every fiber of my being.

Bobbi was the last thing I thought of at night and the first thing I thought of in the morning. I wrote poetry for the first time in my life. Words flowed from me like lava from a volcano. I was a veritable windstorm of literary images. Passages were created from thin air and transferred onto hitherto blank pages. I had no idea where they sprung from. Nor did I care. All that mattered was the all-encompassing passion of my creative self for this delicious creature. I had tapped into an energy that pulsed through my body like electricity through power lines. It had no beginning and no end. I was connected to the transformational essence of my basic being.

No rational explanation could be offered for my inspiration. And none was needed. It was sufficient unto itself. I found a thousand different ways to express my feelings. Words poured forth like water over Niagara Falls. It was an all-encompassing, invisible force with an unimaginable power. I had the strength of ten armies, totally invincible and at the same time unseen and unpredictable. It took on a life of its own. I was merely the messenger, the inspired scribe through which all magnificence flowed. It was a miracle to behold. I could die happy.

A Breakthrough

In early July, Dr. Youngberg decided I was strong enough to get out of bed and into a wheelchair. It was the equivalent of sprouting wings. I was mobile and could propel myself into every corner of the hospital. I could visit any patient in the entire institution. And I did. The weeks of confinement left me with a thirst for new company.

I quickly became an omni-present whirlwind. My arm strength increased the more I pushed myself down the corridor of my floor, onto the elevator and down the hallways of all the other floors of the building. My speed increased rapidly as I pushed the limits of my endurance. I timed myself as I powered through the floors, attempting to set new speed records each day. Progress was rapid. In short order, I could outrace anyone on foot. I attempted to become a virtual blur, dashing from one unit to another.

Although my left arm was still half the size of the right, it was substantially stronger than it had been just a few weeks earlier. The progress encouraged me to work harder at the weight training offered by my physical therapist. While my upper body developed at a hearty rate, the same could not be said for the lower half, especially my left leg which had withered to mere skin and bone.

I began to wonder about my future mobility and whether I could return to school in the fall. It was amply clear that I would not be able to pursue my dream of playing varsity football. What was not so clear was whether I would be able to walk at all.

My roommate, Eddie, was told in no uncertain terms that he would not ever be moving about on his lower limbs. The best he could hope for would be a wheelchair existence. He took this diagnosis with great aplomb.

I admired his quiet confidence and good humor. "I guess this is one opponent I won't be knocking out," he said with a smile. "I guess I'll just have to concentrate on becoming the world's greatest lover. After all, my dick is still intact."

I delayed asking Dr. Youngberg his opinion regarding my own ability to walk for fear of getting the wrong answer. As long as my strength was returning, that was plenty of encouragement for me. I simply presumed that everything would turn out well.

Dad called occasionally from one town or another on the road. He had shown me how to substitute worthless metal slugs for quarters on public phones. Real quarters had a distinctive sound which the operator could recognize. However, if you banged the telephone box with your fist each time a coin was deposited it blurred the distinction and the slugs were taken for the real thing. It also helped to keep up a constant line of chatter with the operator as the required charges were apparently being dropped into the coin slots. I recognized the scam as soon as I heard his voice. "Did you get that operator? How much more do you need? Are you able to hear me OK?" Each question was accompanied by a deposit and a solid smack on the box.

When he got on the line, he told me not to get depressed about my condition. He said I should try to keep my spirits up and not think too much about my disability. I felt awful after his calls. I was NOT depressed or dispirited until he brought up the subject. In all the countless hours I spent on the phone with Mom, she never brought up any of those subjects. It was simply not necessary. He, on the other hand, managed to bring me down in a two-minute conversation by saying all the wrong things. I dreaded his disgusting calls.

My life, in fact, was going exceedingly well. Eddie kept up a constant stream of advice on how to handle women. It was clear he knew because he had a never-ending line of them passing through. They all thought they were his only girlfriend and didn't know about the others. He juggled them as well as the jester on the carnival midway, arranging visits according to his own schedule.

Bobbi was now coming to visit me on a regular basis. Our romance had blossomed into a full-blown infatuation. It was fabulous having someone in my life. It was an ideal relationship. I had no idea how impossible it would be to maintain, nor did I care.

I was happy to be at White Memorial instead of at my home in the projects. It occurred to me that the name "Ramona Gardens" was the only thing beautiful about that crummy public housing complex. It was an irony that had not made an impression on me before. The hospital was everything my home was not—clean, safe and filled with considerate people. It was a great treat to be there.

Mom visited every chance she could. I think she too was relieved to get out of the ghetto. It was the closest we had ever been. Our relationship grew and became a source of great satisfaction to me. I loved my baby sister who was growing into an adorable little girl. My brother delighted in jumping onto my wheelchair and buzzing around the rooftop of the hospital where we spent most of our time.

As July slid into August, my thoughts turned to autumn and returning to school. It was time for me to ask some pointed questions of the good doctor. Would I be able to return to Lincoln? What would my life be like after the hospital? And, most importantly, would I be able to walk under my own power?

While I was not anxious to leave my cloistered life where all my needs were met with gracious generosity, I knew that day would come soon. I could not imagine what awaited me on the outside. But I missed school and the opportunity to return to my studies.

I was well aware that my dreams of playing varsity football would remain just that, dreams. It was a bitter pill to swallow. After playing first string on the JV team, I now figured I would sit on the bench in my junior year on the varsity but hopefully start as a senior.

It was clear that was not to be. Still, I was becoming itchy to get back to my beloved campus. I was going to be 16 in June and had thoughts of getting my first car. I could get a permit at fifteen and a half. That was just a few months away. I had no idea where the money to purchase a car would come from, but I had confidence I could figure it out.

When I finally sat down to talk with Dr. Youngberg, he was very guarded in his predictions for my future. Yes, I would be leaving the hospital in time for the fall semester, but walking was another story altogether. He told me not to plan on it. There was a good chance I might never be able to walk normally again.

This was a possibility I refused to accept. I was confident that it was just a matter of time, strength training, and unwavering determination to get back on my feet. It was one thing to be happy cruising the hospital in a wheelchair, but another thing entirely to think about traveling about the city that way.

When Dr. Youngberg suggested moving me from the wheelchair onto crutches, I was delighted. I saw it as the first step to total recovery even though he warned that the transition would not be easy.

He was right. Crutches were painful and considerably slower than the wheelchair. It took a great deal of practice to get comfortable on them. I worked harder than ever to recover the use of my left leg. The right one was fine, but I could not imagine hopping on one foot to get around. I needed them both.

By the end of August, I felt I was ready to try my first steps without the crutches. It was a mistake. I fell and bruised my arm and upper thigh. The doctor had told me NOT to try that until he approved, but I was stubborn. I felt that if I could manage just one step under my own power, it would be a positive sign of things to come.

It was early September when I successfully negotiated that first step. I was exhilarated, excited, and exhausted all at the same time. I fell on the second step but was able to avoid injury. I was on my way to full recovery. At least, in my own head.

I had not thought to question who was paying the many thousands of dollars invested in my health care and lengthy recovery. I learned the entire tab was being picked up by the March of Dimes. I was deeply grateful and decided to become rich enough one day to repay them in full. I hoped that I could make some other victim of polio as comfortable as I had been. As far as I was concerned, I could not have had better care even if my dad had been a millionaire. I would never forget that charitable organization and the kindness of the Seventh-Day Adventists.

As it happened, the Salk vaccine soon prevented the disease so effectively that I was among the very last to contract it. The March of Dimes terminated its polio operations and turned its efforts to the prevention and treatment of birth defects. It's difficult to express my undying gratitude for their generous assistance. I shall never forget them, Dr. Youngberg, or the staff at White Memorial.

Back to the Barrio

When I returned to the projects nothing had changed, except I was getting around on crutches. With no friendly nurses to bring me meals, no therapist to put me through my drills, and no doctor to look to for advice and support, I was really on my own. It was a major shock to my system.

And, of course, it was impossible to invite Bobbi to come to Ramona Gardens to visit me. My budding love life began to dissipate almost immediately in the light of this new reality. There was a certain romance to being in the hospital. Like a World War II fighter pilot shot down. A hero. But in Ramona Gardens, I was just another poor kid with a bad leg.

My physical condition required a new adjustment to every phase of my former life. I could not go to the market, walk to school, or work for extra money. I spent countless hours on the cement floor of the apartment practicing the workout provided by the hospital. Only the occasional roach stopped to watch in curiosity.

Going to school and getting back home were major efforts. Traveling from one class to another required going up and down stairs, which was like challenging Mt. Everest three times a day. Life on wooden sticks was still new to me, and I was not very good at it. I was often late to class, bringing unwanted attention on myself when I hobbled in. I still had no friends and lived my life in a solitary bubble. Whenever I fell, everyone suddenly got interested in their schoolbooks.

Instead of trying out for varsity football like my old JV teammates, I was assigned to "corrective" gym class. Corrective was another name for "loser." Only the most physically and mentally messed-up students were condemned to that particular realm. All the outcasts in school were enrolled in that forlorn class and I was the lamest of the lot.

Because I had to take the school bus to and from the Gardens, I could not participate in after-school activities. As an eleventh grader there were now school dances, social events and car clubs all of which were off limits to me. Needless to say, dating was out of the question. Not that there were any girls I could ask out anyway.

Only the Delgado household welcomed me. The girls were still my friends and Mama was her same, gracious self. I spent hours there every day. It was my refuge, and I took full advantage of it. I began to look like them with salsa stains on my shirt and chili peppers on my breath. I ate almost every meal with them, participated in planning for upcoming fiestas and generally spent as much time as possible in their messy apartment. They were a godsend.

At Lincoln, I participated in the chess club activities at noon in the classroom of Mr. Avakian. He was a nice guy who treated me well, probably because I was the best chess player in the group. He also fit into Lincoln about as well as I did. When he had an open hour, he would occasionally summon me to his room to play chess with him. He boldly, and quite illegally, pulled me out of class to do that. It was an unexpected treat that meant a lot to me.

I wished I could open up and tell him about my tortured home life, but we were not that close, and I don't know what he would have done with the information. Actually, there was nothing he COULD have done, except perhaps adopt me and I didn't think that was a real possibility. Besides, I could never abandon my little brother and baby sister to the junkie underworld we were living in. I was the only one there to protect them. Avakian was a good guy, but there was a limit as to what I could expect. Nevertheless, he provided much needed companionship as well as intellectual challenge that I valued deeply.

After countless hours of exercising, I was nearly able to take a few steps with the use of a cane. I was exhilarated when that happened. It meant that I might be able to phase out the crutches at some point if I continued to improve. It spurred me on and I doubled, then redoubled, my strength program. With visions of walking playing in my head, I focused on that goal with a fresh determination. If I had it within my control to get back the use of my legs I was damn sure I could make it happen.

It was the most difficult physical task I had ever encountered. My left leg seemed determined not to cooperate. It was just a stick of an appendage with most of the muscle absent. I viewed it with dismay but not without hope. I knew the destroyed muscle would never return, but I didn't know how much healthy tissue remained. I chose to believe there was enough left to accomplish my goal.

It became an obsession with me. I worked out day and night. If my recalcitrant leg could be willed to perform adequately, no power in the world could stop me. I was on a mission.

As 1956 moved into late December, my determined efforts began to pay off. Using the cane, I was able to traverse the courtyard to the Delgado's apartment with partial use of my left leg. It was only twenty steps, and I had a severe limp, but it signaled the beginning of a new phase. The culmination of all that hard work resulted in a glimmer of hope for the new year.

I called Bobbi excitedly and told her the big news. She said I was welcome to come to dinner at her house if I could make it across town. This gave me fresh inspiration. I told her I would accept her invitation when I could make it to the bus stop on the other side of Lancaster Hill.

There was no telling how long that would take, however. Still, there was a pot of gold at the end of the rainbow. All I had to do was drag my reluctant leg to get there.

Back on My Feet

Thanks to a Spartan schedule, I was able to give myself the best Christmas gift ever, a trip to the garbage dump to deposit my crutches. I wasn't beyond needing them, but I decided I'd rather crawl than use them. From that point forward, there was no looking back. With the assistance of a cane, I was able to hobble around fairly well. I disliked having to use any type of support, but I saw it as simply a transition period. And so it was.

By late February, the cane joined the crutches in the trash bin. I was left with a severe limp that caused me to rapidly run out of gas and required numerous time-outs, resting on the nearest support available, but the handwriting was on the wall. I would be able to walk without assistance at some point soon. The future held out hope for a normal stride. To my way of thinking, it was simply a matter of time, and my continued dedication to a program of intense physical therapy. I began to fantasize about returning to the football team in my senior year.

It was a dream I purposely kept from my doctor because I was well aware he would immediately quash it. I still could barely walk. Running was out of the question. But that's why they call them "dreams," isn't it?

Being back on my feet gave me an enormous boost. I could now consider finding a new after-school job. After so many months of being unproductive, I was chomping at the bit. I was in no shape to make deliveries on a bicycle or mow lawns, so I sought out less physically-demanding employment.

I found it at a movie house in downtown Los Angeles. There were numerous theaters lining both sides of the street on Broadway between Fourth Street and Olympic Blvd. I signed on at the Palace as a ticket taker for the "generous" salary of seventy-five cents per hour, before taxes.

I was issued a moth-eaten old uniform that was two sizes too large and smelled of popcorn and former employees. I was stationed at the main entrance with instructions to take a ticket from each patron, tear it in half, giving one part to the customer and placing the other in a nearby container. That was the entire list of my duties.

It was boring beyond belief, but it gave me an opportunity to practice various exercises on my left leg. I looked at the situation as being paid to rehabilitate my bum wheel. All in all, a pretty good deal.

The best part of the job was being close to the candy girls who worked the counter just a few feet from the main entry. They were older than me but still young and quite attractive. During the movie times, there was little activity either at the front door or at the refreshment stand. With so little going on, the girls and I had ample time to communicate and share our life experiences.

Talking to them was the only relief from the unending boredom of just standing there like a statue. My entire job could have been performed just as well by a trained seal. With the girls to talk to, the hours passed quite tolerably.

That pleasant pastime came to a crashing halt when I was informed that I wouldn't be permitted to talk to anyone on the job. My manager stated in no uncertain terms that I was not allowed to converse with the other employees under any conditions.

I ignored his warning and continued on just as I had in the past. Unfortunately, the girls had also been warned and dropped our communications forthwith. It was no problem for them, since they could talk to each other. I, on the other hand, had only myself to talk to. Since I was pretty sure of what I had to say, I mainly grumbled out loud. One day my boss passed by and inquired as to what I was saying. Unwisely, I told him I hated this fucking job and he should stick it up his ass.

The next day, I found new employment at the State Theatre down the street. It was the same drill, except the candy counter was not located near the entrance and there was no opportunity to converse with anyone. After a few weeks of crushing boredom, I quit and moved over to the Orpheum. I discovered that I could work at any theatre I chose, mainly because no one wanted a stifling, go-nowhere job, and they were always on the lookout for new help. Eventually, I worked at a dozen different venues.

I finally found a permanent home at the Los Angeles Theatre. The reason I was able to stick it out there was because of the manager, a good-looking, if slightly sleazy, Italian guy named

Victor Bugliosi. He hated his job almost as much as I hated mine, but he was the big cheese there and could do as he pleased. Mainly what pleased him was to take one of the candy girls into the darkened projection room and instruct them on the finer points of managing a theater.

Vic and I got along well because he needed someone to cover for him when he was missing in action, while I had the freedom to roam the theater whenever I was not needed at the front door. In addition, I was allowed to work as an usher instead of taking tickets. What that meant was that after people were seated, I was free to watch the movie, practice my leg exercises, or goof off as I chose. It worked out well for both of us.

One day, he mentioned that his brother, Vincent, was coming to visit him at work. He was very proud of his brother who was just getting out of the Navy and planned a career in law. He told me Vince was an exceptionally bright guy aside from being an "arrogant asshole." At the time, neither of us would have imagined that Vincent would later achieve dubious notoriety as the prosecutor in the Charles Manson murder trial.

Vic's description of his brother was right on. When Vince arrived at the theater, he was dressed neat as a pin and had an attitude of unmatched superiority. He had an exceptional ability to look right through you and let you know how entirely worthless you were, without ever saying a word. He declined to shake my hand when we were introduced.

I had never felt such disdain up close and I made a mental note to avoid him whenever he returned. It was hard for me to believe there were such self-centered jerks in the world, but there it was in front of me. While I could not figure out what made people act like that, I guessed that it probably derived from an inner insecurity. Better to act outwardly superior than allow people to see how utterly frightened you are.

By 11:00 or 11:30 in the evening, I got off work and caught the Sierra Vista bus back to the projects. There was no direct service into Ramona Gardens. It was clear that people at the bottom of the economic ladder deserved only scorn from the public bus company. The driver dropped me at Soto and Lancaster, a full half-mile from my house. I limped over Lancaster hill and arrived home exhausted.

The Borscht Belt

At last the day came when I felt strong enough take Bobbi up on her offer to come to dinner. I dressed in my best slacks and shirt, which I had recently purchased with my earnings from the Los Angeles Theatre.

It required four bus changes and over three hours to get from the projects in East L.A. to the Fairfax district in West L.A., a journey that took about a half-hour by car.

The businesses on Fairfax were bannered with signs letting you know you had entered the Jewish neighborhood of the city. Hebrew lettering announced kosher restaurants and butcher shops. Religious stores carried large supplies of menorahs, yartzheit holy candles, and jewelry with Jewish icons. Old men in skull caps, dressed in long black coats, peered into the bakeries and delicatessens lining the boulevard. Old ladies wearing scarves around their heads sat on bus benches, kvetching in Yiddish with much arm waving and expressions of old world camaraderie.

Canter's restaurant was filled to overflowing with people crowding the entrance and spilling out onto the sidewalk waiting to be seated. The smell of fresh rye bread, pickled herring, latkes, and hot pastrami all rolled into one big knish wafted onto the road.

Down the street, youngsters filed into the local yeshiva to study their Hebrew lessons. Some were dressed exactly like the old orthodox men, all in black with their hair trailing in curls down both sides of their face.

By the time I reached Bobbi's house, I was limping noticeably and my leg was painfully beginning to cramp up. I put on a brave smile and knocked on the door which had a mezuzah strategically located above the doorbell.

Bobbi answered the door, looking radiant as ever. Instantly, I forgot the pain in my leg, the multiple bus rides, and the hours in transit. For that moment everything was perfect.

It was the first time I had ever seen her outside the hospital. She gave me just the slightest hint of a hug, then escorted me into the living room where her parents and older sister

Annette were waiting.

Bobbi's father and mother were seated on a couch and I was positioned into an armchair opposite them. Bobbi and Annette exited the room and left us alone. I felt like the inquisition was about to begin and that the judgment and sentencing were a foregone conclusion. I waited for the executioner to appear, slip a black bag over my head, and swing the axe.

It was a torturous grilling. None of the questions they asked me had easy answers. "So what does your father do?" inquired her Mom. I had to think a moment. I didn't think that saying, "Oh, he's a carnival thief who sells heroin in the off season," was a very good answer. Instead I said, "He's in sales." I didn't offer any details, hoping they'd let it drop. No such luck. "Really, what KIND of sales?" she pried. I hemmed and hawed, "Oh, different seasonal items. He's really busy around Christmas time, with specialty gift items."

Her Dad wanted to know, "So where do you live?" I replied, "East Los Angeles." He furrowed his brow and asked. "Why do you live there?" I responded, "Housing is more affordable, I think." He pursued his interrogation, "So is there still a Jewish community out there? Which temple do you belong to?" I thought, "How about Our Lady of Perpetual Poverty," but said, "The old Breed Street Temple," which I had passed on my delivery route for the butcher. He thought a moment, then challenged me. "I thought that was closed." Thinking on my feet I answered, "Oh, it is for the moment, but they're going to reopen soon." He stroked his chin, "Really, I thought it was closed for good. I'm glad to hear they will be reopening."

Bobbi's Mom rescued me by noting that dinner was ready and we should all move towards the dining room. They served brisket of beef which was delicious. I had never eaten it before. Mom served mainly meatloaf or macaroni and cheese at home. Bobbi and her sister spoke to each other during the meal, occasionally giggling. I was getting more uncomfortable by the minute.

I sensed things were going from bad to worse. At that point all I wanted was to bolt for the front door.

Her Mom asked me if I would like something to drink. I said, "Sure, how about some milk?" The whole room went silent as though I had requested a scotch on the rocks. "You drink milk with meat?" her mother asked incredulously. "Well, yeah, I guess." Her father grumbled, "I never heard of such a thing." The two parents began whispering to each other furiously. At last her mother said, "Fine. If he wants milk, he can have milk." She left the room. Bobbi leaned over and said, "Jews don't drink milk with meat." This was news to me. I probably should have crossed myself and said three 'Hail Marys' which I had learned from my days of selling Sunday papers at the Catholic church.

The rest of the evening was a blur, consisting of more probing questions and unsatisfying answers. I began longing for the safety of the projects and the comfort of the Delgados' living room.

By the time I limped home late that night, I had lost any desire I might have had for life on the Westside. I wished I could have spent some alone time with Bobbi, but I could see no way that was going to happen. This wasn't like the good ol' days at the hospital.

I reluctantly concluded that I was just a kid from the barrio and had no real control over my life. It was heartbreaking, but it was real.

An Inspiration

By early 1957, while I was still a junior, I had arranged my life so that I spent almost no time at home. School consumed my days, and I went to work directly afterwards. The only time I was inside our miserable dwelling was to sleep. By the time I got home, I was so exhausted even the all-night raging battles over who got the most heroin didn't keep me up. I was living a solitary life and it was just fine with me. No one asked where I was or what I did with my time. I could have joined the French Foreign Legion, been gone for years, and not one person would have noticed.

I still saved my meager wages, looking forward to the day I could purchase my first car. I had completed a driver's training course during the first semester and received a conditional license. All that was left was to find an automobile I could afford.

While my time spent at Lincoln was still the highlight of my existence, I noted a considerable lack of interest in studies by the general student body. Only a handful of my classmates had plans to go to college and were concentrating on academic subjects.

For the most part, kids were just passing time and getting by with the least effort possible. Intentionally acquiring good grades was actually cause for inviting open hostility and catcalls referring to me as an ass-kisser.

My social studies teacher was an energetic, former Lincoln graduate, named Raymond Lopez. Each day Mr. Lopez entered the classroom with armfuls of teaching aids that he had amassed over the years. He had charts, photos, articles, book reviews, and every imaginable type of extra-curricular document. He was an unending fount of pure inspiration. He had a vast knowledge of music, history, and some subjects I hadn't even heard of.

Out of 30 students, only those in the front row paid any attention. There was myself, Patricia Joe, Esther Arakaki, Armando Lujan (who was later to become the first Mexican admitted to West Point), and Sandra Bonnano, editor of the school newspaper. The rest of the class talked, passed notes, and shot rubber bands at each other. The classroom looked like pandemonium to the casual observer. But for those of us up close, it was an opportunity to learn from the most dedicated teacher one could ever encounter.

It wasn't only WHAT Mr. Lopez taught but the WAY he presented it. He was the most enthusiastic individual I had ever met in person. He produced prodigious flurries of words as he pulled one illustration after another from his educational bag of tricks. His arms waved about like windmills, pointing out the curious and the obscure. Constantly in motion, he had a continuous supply of high energy as well as copious learning materials.

There was never enough time to cover all the subjects Ray brought with him. He always left me hungering for more. If I thought I could pick up on the balance of what he had to offer during the next class I was wrong. The following day he would have an entirely new set of goodies for us. It was impossible to keep up with him.

What was perhaps even more amazing, he had different armfuls of materials for the next incoming class. He must have spent countless hours preparing for each day. He let nothing slow him down. Not unruly students, classroom noise, or physical exhaustion. He set a standard far beyond the capability of ordinary mortals.

Each time I left his classroom, I was incredibly energized for the rest of the day. He set off a spark in me that ignited a thirst for knowledge and a respect for learning far beyond what I believed possible. And he did it all with great humor and an infectious smile that lit up the entire room. He was simply the eighth wonder of the world.

Ray Lopez, plain and simple, changed my life. Just to see an individual with such energy, devotion, and good will was a revelation in itself. I had no idea people could be like that. He was extraordinary in every sense of the word. He was totally devoted to his calling, which was to make the maximum amount of educational material available to his students. Whether they picked up on it, understood what he was doing, or even gave a damn was beside the point.

He was intent on doing his job and no force on earth could deter him. Just amazing.

A Lesson in Humility

My miserly habits paid off when I had an opportunity to get a set of wheels for a hundred bucks. One of my buddies at work had a 1940 Ford for sale. It was pretty ratty, but it ran, and I knew we had an auto shop at school which worked on student vehicles. I planned to take the car directly to the shop and ask the teacher if he could use it as a repair demo to instruct the students. It was my chance to drop public transportation and become independent. It would save me at least two hours a day in travel time.

I took the wreck to the instructor who graciously agreed to use it for educational purposes and parked it in the rear of the garage. I would have to wait until the guys in the class finished working on their own cars before they got to it. But I had waited this long, so a little longer would be no problem.

Weeks went by and they never got around to working on the car. I was getting antsy, but I tried to be patient. At last they started to go through the vehicle and see what it needed. More weeks elapsed. When repairs actually began, it was one delay after another. Each time I checked out the progress, I was told that there were unforeseen difficulties causing more delays.

I realized it was just a high school automotive shop, but it was becoming an unending project. I started going to check on it daily but still nothing ever seemed to get done. My frustration level was going through the roof. My great purchase was becoming a royal pain-in-the-ass. I began to regret the whole deal. I wished I had my hundred dollars back.

One day after school, I went out to the shop to see if any progress had been made. Everyone had gone home except the instructor. He shook his head when I inquired as to whether any headway had been made on my car.

Then he invited me into his small office and said, "May I speak to you freely?" I had no idea what he might say. We had never spoken before and I had not taken one of his classes. I answered, "Sure. What's up?" He spoke softly. "It's not easy for me to say this, but I feel I should say something."

189

He shifted uneasily in his chair and continued, "Your car was finished weeks ago. But each time I was about to call you in to pick it up, one of the students intentionally broke another part or tore out some wires."

I shook my head in disbelief. "B, but, how could that be?" I stammered. He leaned forward and said, "They hate you. I'm not sure why. You seem like a decent enough kid to me. But I can tell you there have been repeated efforts to sabotage your car."

I sat in stunned silence. Suddenly all the delays made sense. They were not trying to fix the car, they were trying to destroy it. I could feel blood rushing to my head. I was angrier than I could ever remember. I was ready to kill somebody.

He continued, "I don't think it's your fault, but they believe you come off as a snob. They think you're stand-offish and act like you're better than they are. It may be because you get good grades. It may be for some other reason. I don't know. You don't appear that way to me, but I can assure you that's the way they see you."

I asked him, "What do you think I should do?" He replied, "I'd like you to read a book. It's called *How to Win Friends and Influence People* by Dale Carnegie."

He wrote the title down on a piece of paper and handed it to me. "Just read it. There's good advice in there and I think it may help you get along better. In the meantime, I will see to it that your car is fixed and returned to you."

I had no interest in getting the assholes in his class to like me, but I agreed to read the book anyway. I borrowed it from the library the next day and read it cover to cover. It was full of suggestions on how to listen, how to talk to people and how to behave. It seemed phony and strained to me, but I decided to try it out anyway.

In the following months, I was elected to the school Senate, accepted into a popular car club, had two good friends and was nominated for student body President.

A Public Life

My first close friend was an Italian kid named Joe Criscione. Born in Benghazi, Libya, Joe had immigrated to the U.S. with his family when he was 12 years old. Although he spoke no English when he arrived on America's shores, he picked up the language easily and within a couple of years had not even a trace of an accent. Joe was bright, easy going, and had a winning smile. He was a good student who played on the basketball team, worked weekends at a screen installation company and participated in student government. He was also good-looking and garnered much attention from the girls in school.

Best of all, we clicked immediately and found we had similar interests. We were both huge fans of Frank Sinatra, Dean Martin, and Ella Fitzgerald. We spent countless hours spinning records in his room while ogling the photos in Playboy magazines he kept secreted in his closet.

On Friday afternoons, his mom made the best pizza on the face of the earth for her family, consisting of Joe's dad who worked on the railroad, his older brother, younger brother, and two sisters. Mama's pizza dough covered every square inch of the kitchen. Although it is impossible to describe the taste, I can say that it was the most outrageously delicious dish I had ever tasted in my life. When I left the house, his mom piled me high with slices to bring home to my family. Because I was so full when I left his house, the homemade pizza actually made it back to the projects where my family would be anxiously waiting at the door for their weekly treat. It ruined me for commercial pizza for the rest of my life.

My other buddy was Bob Dilworth, a fair-haired WASP, one of the few at Lincoln. He lived nearby the school in a large old clapboard house with his mother. He was an outstanding trumpet player in the school band and took private lessons as well. A popular guy, I was surprised that he included me in his life, often spending afternoons with me at his pad just hanging out and talking to neighborhood girls. His mom accepted me with some reservations. She told Bob that I was OK, but had "...too much personality."

At this time, I began to take an interest in public speaking. It was an activity that drew little attention from anyone else in the student body, leaving me as the sole participant in inter-school competitions representing Abraham Lincoln High School. Within a short period of time, I was entering speech contests across the city. I took to the podium like I had been preparing for it my whole life. I loved standing up in front of large crowds who were there to listen to ME.

It was not that I had anything to say. I had no cause or driving desire to communicate an idea. It was the pure joy of addressing a large gathering of people, the undiluted thrill of being the center of attention. The spotlight on me, ears attuned to my words, my actions, my gestures, the undeniable excitement of stardom—I was a ham, through and through.

This development came as a surprise. I had no clue I had the inspiration to be a budding orator. Since there was zero interest in either the faculty or the student body, I was left to my own devices. I researched the library for notices of upcoming events. I scanned local and citywide newspapers and read newsletters from local service clubs like Kiwanis, Rotary and Lions. They each had in-house competitions I could sign up for.

The school excused me from classes to attend these events. Thus, in the middle of the day I might find myself out and about the city cruising to a speech venue in my now functioning '40 Ford. Neither administrators nor teachers had the slightest idea how long I needed to be away from school to complete each contest, so I was pretty much on my own time schedule.

I usually left campus earlier than necessary and had breakfast at the Pantry Cafe downtown with the morning business crowd. I tried to imagine what life was like having a real job. What did people do without school?

After the speech competition, I'd cruise the Main Street bars, poking my head inside the smelly, dark, boozy taverns, ogling the sleazy B-girls seated on high stools, beckoning to passersby. I longed to go inside but somehow knew instinctively I was better off venturing no further than the front door. Still, the half-dressed floozies captured my teenage imagination. What kind of women were they? What forbidden pleasures did they offer? Where did they do it? How much did they charge?

Unfortunately, I would not find out.

Politics

Towards the end of my junior year, I was approached by some students who suggested that I consider becoming a candidate in the upcoming election to select the student body President for the following school year. I had been elected to the school Senate, which was the first official office I had ever held in my life. It was largely a position with no real significance or power, and I only represented my homeroom, but I did get close to those students who had some interest in the political process. They encouraged me to open a full-on campaign.

My opponent would surely be Armando "Army" Lujan, a formidable foe. Army was quarterback on the football team, commander of the Abraham Lincoln R.O.T.C. and one of the brightest kids in school. In addition, he was a personal friend. We both belonged to the Nomads Car Club and proudly wore our signature three-quarter length gray coats with the club insignia on the back.

It never occurred to me that I would stand a chance in a school-wide election against the premier Mexican student in a primarily Mexican high school. I took up the subject with my Mom. "You can do anything you want," she told me. "I have complete confidence in you. I've never seen you fail at anything you set your mind to. Just go for it."

That was it. She ended the conversation and returned to the kitchen where she was making the evening meal. I was left to consider her unwavering confidence. I thought, "That's easy for you to say."

With no one else to consult, I told my supporters in the school Senate that I would run. They responded enthusiastically and began immediately to plan the campaign strategy. They formed a Platform Committee to determine what my message was to be, an Art Committee to design and prepare posters and banners to be displayed throughout the campus, and an Outreach Committee to muster informal support among the student body. I was overwhelmed by their organizational efficiency.

They put me to work writing a speech to be delivered at

193

a general assembly of the student body in the school auditorium the day before the election, in which all of the candidates for office were given a chance to be heard. This was right up my alley, in light of my recent public speaking successes. My speech went over well, without a single catcall.

The day of the election, I was all nerves. I sat in classes, not hearing a single word the teachers said. I began to regret having run for office at all. It wasn't really my idea, and I feared the embarrassment of being trounced. In addition to all of my other insecurities, I was aware that Lincoln had never elected a student body President from the projects. By the end of the school day, I was an emotional mess.

Towards the afternoon, during fifth period, a messenger came into out social studies class and handed a note to the teacher. She read the note to herself then said, "Class, I have the results of the student body elections for officers for next year." I held my breath and stared at the dust specks on my desk as she read the victors for the various offices.

At last she stated, "And our student body President for 1958 is...KENNY KAHN!" She smiled broadly at me and invited me to stand and accept a rousing round of applause from my classmates. The blood rushed to my head as I rose.

It was incomprehensible. I had WON! The reality was overwhelming. Then she continued, "Kenny received a majority of votes in every homeroom in school. This is a first in Lincoln history." I was mobbed by kids slapping me on the back and wishing me good luck.

At an impromptu celebration party at a local taco stand down the street, my comrades told me how the great victory happened. One said, "They thought Army was too high and mighty, that he needed to be knocked down a bit." Another added, "Mexicans don't appreciate it when someone acts like they're too good for you. They wanted to take him down." I was shocked because I never viewed my friend Army like that. He was one of the "best and brightest" of my classmates and a regular guy who was down with a popular car club. I guess I was wrong. Either way, it was fairly clear that the electorate was not so much voting FOR me, as expressing displeasure over my opponent. I guess he should've read *How to Win Friends and Influence People.*

When I returned to the projects late that afternoon and told my Mom, she gave me a hug and said, "I told you, you could do it." That was it. Nothing more. I then dashed over to the Delgados for a victory party that they were all too happy to provide.

Each of the girls lined up to give me a luscious hug and kiss. I was in heaven. They told me how great a victory it was and that, "It's about time someone from Ramona Gardens became President."

Mama Delgado sent the girls out to the store to pick up the makings for a huge fiesta. That night, we danced and feasted and hugged until the early morning hours.

Senior Year

After another summer on the road with my family, I came home early to prepare for the fall semester in 1957. Although I still walked with a slight limp, I had fantasies of going out for the football team.

I went to visit Dr. Youngberg and he was pleased with my progress, but when I made mention of playing ball, he came down on me hard. "Absolutely not. You should be grateful you can walk. Competitive sports are out of the question. Especially football. I don't want you to even bring the subject up again."

I left his office dejected but not deterred. I knew this would be my last chance to play the game I loved. I was certainly no candidate for any college level sports.

I worked out on my own, day and night, to try to get into shape. On the first day of football practice, I showed up at the coach's office and asked for a private meeting with him. He agreed and invited me in.

"Hi Kenny, what's up?" he inquired. "I want to try out for the team," I replied. He laughed, "Surely, you're joking. You were in corrective P.E. last year recovering from polio. How could I possibly let you come out for football? There's no way."

I made my pitch. "Coach, I've been working out with weights all summer. I've made tremendous improvements. Just give me a chance. I'll understand if you cut me. Please. It's important to me."

He shook his head emphatically. "I couldn't even begin to consider it without a note from your doctor. And even then, it would be doubtful."

I thanked him for his time and departed. I had a plan. I went back to the doctor for another visit. I arrived over the noon hour when I knew his secretary would be out for lunch. While alone in the waiting room, I shuffled through her desk. I found what I was looking for: a blank piece of the doctor's personal stationery. I took a few sheets and slipped them into my notebook, then knocked on the doctor's door and announced myself.

When he answered the door, he appeared to be a bit perplexed. "Do you have an appointment?" he said. I told him I was just in the neighborhood and simply dropped in to say hi. He accepted my explanation and invited me in for a brief meeting. We talked for a few minutes during which I expressed my appreciation for all his help, then we shook hands and I departed. The plan was working.

I took the blank sheets to school and used an available machine in one of the typing classes. I wrote a letter giving me permission to participate in the football program. Then I forged the doctor's signature and brought the letter to Coach Leckman.

When I showed the letter to Coach, he snorted, "I don't give a damn what some fool doctor says, YOU CAN'T PLAY FOOTBALL." His tirade blew me back three steps. "But Coach," I protested, "I'm not asking you to let me 'PLAY' football. Just let me work out with the team until the real hitting starts. If I'm not in condition you can cut me then."

He stroked his cheek thoughtfully. "Hmmm, maybe," he said slowly, but then added in a no-nonsense tone, "you keep up with EVERY drill or you're outta here? Understood?"

"Yessir." I saluted smartly. "Understood."

Coach then squinted his eyes and gave me an unmistakable look that said, "I know what's going on here." Instead he said, "I can see how you got elected." I offered a weak smile as I backed obsequiously out of the room. As I turned to leave he shouted out, "And don't think for one minute that I believe that horseshit official doctor's letter."

September Mourn

So that was how I found myself huffing and puffing around the track on the outside of the football field in the sweltering Indian summer. I was overcome by heat and exhaustion. We were only running two laps, a half-mile, but I became pretty convinced that I would never make it after the first lap.

My tongue was hanging out, I was turning red and gasping for air. Perspiration covered my body. My left leg felt disconnected from my body. Consequently, my right leg overcompensated and I began to noticeably limp on my left side while cramping up on my right side.

I was beginning to pray for death. A quick end seemed like my best hope. Luckily, there were a few other real slow, overweight guys who were beginning to fade as well. They were all ahead of me but still within sight. I could pretend that I was running with them as a group and hope Coach wouldn't notice.

My body was rebelling in a big time way at this point. On the other hand, it didn't matter much since I had left my body some time ago and was being driven onward by my semi-fried brain. For some inexplicable reason, it was allowing me to just keep on keepin' on.

When I finally stumbled across the finish line, I was a good twenty yards behind the last man, the 280-pound tackle, Covarrubias, who had stopped at the half-way point to take a whiz on the track. I collapsed on the ground in a heap, but was still conscious. I had survived the first big test. Yahoo! Coach acted like he never noticed.

The workouts didn't get any easier after that first day. On the other hand, they never got any worse. I accumulated just enough confidence to begin to believe I could stick it through. I suffered horribly each night and got little sleep.

It was not a happy time. My limp was exaggerated during the school day from the aftereffects of the practice from the day before. I dragged my left leg from one class to another. There was not one moment when I wasn't feeling pain in one body part or another. Still, I maintained a blind faith that one day it would begin to subside. I would accept no less. I knew it in my bones that I would see this thing out.

I couldn't really say I was having fun, but I was definitely getting a certain satisfaction from going out to the practice field each day and butting heads with my teammates.

Although I never played all year, I still got to ride the team bus to all the games, joke with the guys and watch the game from the bench. There were several night games and quite a few fans in attendance. It felt good just to go onto the field for pre-game warm-ups in front of the student body. While we lost most of our games that year, the guys took pride in the fact that we never lost a fight in the stands.

58

An Expanding Universe

My life was on a fast-track for the first time. Between student government, football practice, and public speaking events, my days were booked solid.

There were still classes to complete but I barely noticed them. I was missing-in-action most of the time. Since no one on the teaching staff had complete knowledge of my activities, I was able to leave class whenever I wished. I would stand up and announce to the teacher, "I have an event to attend," or "I'm needed for a meeting." Then I would simply exit stage left. I also had complete freedom to leave campus, jump into my car and drive off. It was all cool with the powers-that-be.

There were, in fact, unending "leadership conferences" hosted by different sponsors held at various locations around the city, and indeed, around the state. I attended them all. They repeatedly told us that we were the cream of the crop and the future leaders of America.

What they didn't mention was that real power in the country was held exclusively by another generation and we would be old and gray before it was our turn. But we were allowed to pretend that we mattered tremendously and were filled with self-importance. Not a pretty picture, looking back, but at the time we thought we were pretty special.

It also gave me an opportunity to observe and compare life on high school campuses in other parts of the city. At Westchester High, all the guys wore white pants. They looked like extras in an Annette Funicello/Frankie Avalon beach party movie. No one at Lincoln wore white pants. Khakis were the order of the day. Anyone in white pants would have been dubbed a sissy.

Also prevalent at these meetings was lots of white skin. The vast majority of "leaders" were Caucasian. The occasional minority student was looked upon as an unusual aberration, almost like a Martian. Since there were so many of these gatherings, everyone soon knew the other "leaders" on a first name basis. It was like belonging to an exclusive country club. Underneath all the posturing and posing, I think we all knew it was just a neat way to skip classes.

The unspoken message of these leadership conferences was that America was basically for white people. Minorities were tolerated and allowed to participate on the edges, but they were just an afterthought. It was necessary to sprinkle in a few to prove how inclusive our society was. Proof to the world that the U.S. was a "melting pot" and open to everyone.

Student Council

As student body President, I presided over all school assemblies, special events and meetings of the Student Council. With little supervision, I began to fool around a bit. I loved to tell jokes, so meetings were often nothing more than me trying out new material on a captive audience.

My buddy, Joe Criscione, had been elected Secretary of Social Affairs, so he planned parties, dances, and other school official gatherings. His position allowed us to be on the ground floor of every event, controlling who was assigned to what task and how they were to be performed.

The best part of our Council was our faculty supervisor, Ray Lopez. He brought an intensity of spirit and enthusiasm that infected us all. Ray was a detail guy who wanted everything to be laid out in specifics. He taught us the importance of comprehensive planning. More than that, he exuded an uncommon commitment to the projects we undertook.

Ray Lopez also had the best attitude of any human I have met before or since. His easy laugh and high-octane energy inspired us all. He made us want to do our best.

Ray fretted that I was way too impulsive for his taste and his approach to events. Instead of sticking to his carefully drawn programs for student assemblies, I blew time schedules by practicing my comedy routines on the student body. They loved it, but Ray had heart palpitations, gesticulating at me wildly from his vantage point off stage. I blithely ignored his pleas to get back to the carefully planned schedule. I didn't want to cause him pain, but I was having such a good time, I figured he'd get over it. I was pretty sure he knew I had a deep affection for him and hopefully, that would make everything OK.

In truth, Ray Lopez was the teacher who made a difference in my life. Other teachers were well-meaning, but Ray was a cut above. He would do anything in his power to enhance the educational level of his students. He would generously share his time whether during a free hour in his daily schedule, after school, or before school at a 7:00 a.m. breakfast meeting. Even weekends were available for meetings.

At a time when many of his students had never even seen the Pacific Ocean, only 20 miles away, Ray would offer to spend a day supervising a trip to the beach.

It was clear he was not in it for the money. No teachers are. But he was an exceptional case. He loved his job, his students, and Abraham Lincoln High School, from which he, himself, had graduated. His dedication surpassed even excellent teachers, and bordered on saintliness. The example he set far exceeded the so-called student "leadership" meetings I attended with their hollow congratulations on our supposedly lofty achievements. His sparkling dedication will live on in me as long as I shall live. I only hope that I might inspire one student as Ray inspired me.

Gangs

As I extended my travels around the Lincoln Heights community, I discovered new neighborhoods to explore. What I found was that each area was dominated by a different local gang. While my home in the Ramona Gardens projects was squarely in the middle of "Big Hazard," the adjoining living space on the other side of Soto Street was home to "Little Hazard," an equally tough group. I had occasion to cross the park in between the two turfs often. I soon learned the ropes and found distinctly different centers of power.

When I played baseball at Downey Park, near the high school, I was introduced to "Clover." A few blocks away was "The Avenues," and closer to downtown was "Dogtown." They were all predominantly Mexican gangs.

Luckily for me, I had now extended my circle of friends and acquaintances to the point where I knew young members of each group. On my numerous ventures outside my home area, I sometimes got trapped by renegade bands of bad-ass street guys. The confrontations were quickly defused when I recognized one or two guys from school. Once I was identified as not belonging to a rival gang, I would be let go unharmed.

This gave me freedom to roam and explore other parts of Lincoln Heights. I saw where the guys lived, what their families looked like and where they hung out.

While the presence of these alleged underworld characters might have been menacing or even life-threatening to outsiders, instead I got a glimpse into a world not often seen by the public. Outside of infrequent gang fights, which I never saw but heard about through the rumor mill, the guys were for the most part very cool.

When I saw them in school, they were open and willing to spend time with me. Many of them were friendly and had a good sense of humor. I passed countless hours just sitting on the broad expanse of green grass in front of the school and bull-shitting about classes, teachers, other students, and life in general.

I found the so-called "gangsters" to be bright, amiable,

and smart. I was just as content to rap with them as with the better, more intellectual students. Probably more.

I never inquired as to exactly how they spent their time after school. It was none of my business and I think they appreciated me for not inquiring. The ultimate conclusion I reached was that they were, for the most part, good guys who I felt privileged to be with.

Because Lincoln Heights is a relatively small neighborhood everybody ran into each other at social events. There were seldom fireworks even when rival gangs encountered each other. Perhaps it was out of respect for the hosts of the various events or just an unspoken rule that physical battles were to be fought at other times and places.

There were, of course, exceptions. I attended a few parties which included an unscheduled knife fight in the back yard. On those occasions, I slipped quickly out the front door. The only close call I ever had personally was at a party where I was getting very romantic with a pretty girl who was clearly encouraging me. We were doing the "dirty bop" and grinding sensuously on the dance floor to slow songs.

Towards the end of the evening, one of my buddies pulled me aside and said, "Her boyfriend just pulled up with a carload of really nasty guys. I suggest you get out of here in a hurry."

I didn't need a second invitation. I snagged my coat, whispered in her ear that "my ride is leaving," and split through a side door. She looked disappointed and started to protest but I didn't look back. In reality, I was more disappointed than her, but I was in no mood for a confrontation with an angry boyfriend. My buddy and I wound up at our usual hangout on Olvera Street, munching taquitos with guacamole. Half of me was still glowing from her heat and the other half was just relieved to have all my body parts in working order.

Back at the Back

Thanks to Coach not cutting me from the football team, I was able to practice after school every day. On Friday game days, I sat on the bench with the other reserves. As the season progressed it became crystal clear, I would not see any playing time. I was forced to deal with cold reality. I was simply not good enough.

I also realized that the team experience consisted mainly of practice sessions. Since the first team needed dummies to beat up on, we were elected. I didn't mind the ass-kickings so much because I actually got to be on the playing field, blocking and tackling with the varsity. It was a vindication in itself. And, I got a picture in the year book with me in full uniform.

My association with the other bench-warmers taught me a valuable lesson...not everyone can be a star. There is a time to star and a time to be part of the chorus. Both are essential and both are respectable. Gridiron glory, such as it is, is fleeting, and by not being a star there were no lofty heights to fall from. We grunts were there for the true love of the game. Our satisfaction came from the practice field. With no hope of playing on game day, practice was our reward. We got into the best physical condition of our lives and made close friendships. That was enough.

After school, I then went directly to work. I drove downtown to the L.A. Theatre, where I donned my moth-eaten uniform and wrinkled shirt, for a five- or six-hour shift. The job was driving me crazy. I could not read or talk to anyone. Even when I became an usher, I could only sit in the last row of the darkened theatre and watch the same movie over and over. I saw Oklahoma eighteen times. I knew every line of every song as well as every facial expression of the actors.

Unfortunately, the job offered my only source of income. Without it, I couldn't buy anything or go anywhere. I had countless hours to contemplate my future. I thought of every possible way to make money. I knew I could have a fairly profitable life on the carnival. After all the years on the road, I had learned to be quite a good thief.

It was an attractive option which my parents wanted me to

take. I viewed it as a chance to break for freedom. After high school, I could work as a carny full time, and, without a doubt, graduate to operating a flat store and make some serious money.

With a flattie's income, I could move out of the hated projects, buy a nice car and get my own place. But I couldn't really imagine a lifetime of dusty, dirty, carnival lots. Besides, what would my little brother and baby sister do without me to protect them?

I finally decided that the only way out was to continue my education as long as possible. I registered for Los Angeles City College. I was scheduled to enter in September 1958. The school was an easy hop from my house and I set up a commuting schedule with my friend Joe. The enrollment fee was six dollars and fifty cents for the semester. That included admission to all school events as well.

The decision was met with indifference by my parents. They were disappointed that I would be wasting more years in school when I could be out earning good money.

Nothing had changed in their lives in the five years we'd lived in Ramona Gardens. Our apartment was still a shooting gallery for the neighborhood junkies. The all-night screaming arguments continued without letup. We were still in debt to Abe at the corner market, and he never gave up his efforts to purchase my little sister.

I still had no one I could confide in. Nobody would understand. Even if they did, there was nothing anyone could do. I was becoming frustrated from all the bottled up anger inside me. From time to time I would begin screaming at the top of my lungs. The outbursts became more pronounced and more frequent as my senior year progressed. I kept the incidents inside my house, never daring to scream in public.

I developed two lives. During the day I was an exemplary student and motivated leader. At night I was a sullen movie theatre usher and screaming maniac. It was a stressful combo.

I could qualify to play both Dr. Jekyll and Mr. Hyde in drama class. No acting required. I was two people. I spent the majority of my life attempting to present a socially-acceptable image to the world. Trying to prove that I was not a product of my parents. The only problem was that this image had nothing to do with reality. My life was one long lie.

And I was getting damn good at it.

High Society

In the Mexican community, there are large celebrations every weekend. Someone was always getting married and throwing a big wedding, or someone was having a "quincinera" and hosting a huge bash, or there was some holiday that called for a giant fiesta. There were a limited number of convenient locations to host these events, so the same ones were used over and over.

On Friday night, you could just cruise over to one of the neighborhood churches to see if someone was throwing a big wedding bash with live music and plenty of food. If there was, you could park across the street and watch the side door. Someone was always ducking out the side for a smoke. When the door opened, you could see inside. If you saw anyone you knew, you could say they invited you. If you were super cool, you could just slide in unnoticed.

If you did not see anyone you knew inside and you just waited for awhile, other professional party crashers would show up. Then you could rap with them from car to car. "Hey, Tony what's up? Can you get us into the hall?" Tony would lean out the window and say, "No, man I don' know nobody here. I can't get myself in."

My buddy Ray, who was at the wheel, called back, "Hey isn't that Nacho at the front door?" Tony turned his head to look, "Yeah, that's him. He sometimes works the door here. He can get us in. I let him cheat on his last math test off my paper, I'm pretty sure he'll do it."

Ray exclaimed, "Hey that's Rosa from my neighborhood, he's letting her in. If she can get in we can."

And we did. Almost always. Ray Hilario was my partner in crime. Every Friday night, we'd scrape together sixty cents for two gallons of gas and then cover every venue. We hit every hot spot in town. Ray and I had a lot in common ... neither of us could get a date. So, by process of elimination, we ended up with each other. Ray came from a solid family with good values. Coming from Montana to settle in California, they had a modest, but well-kept house.

Ray had a good sense of humor and we played off each

other very well. We could keep ourselves amused for hours. Even when things didn't go so well, like when his jalopy would break down and we wound up pushing it all over town.

We developed a full-scale social life with functions of all sorts filling our weekends. One night, we were dancing to the sounds of the Sal Chico Band at a hotel downtown and the next night, dining at a fancy wedding at the Gigi Hall.

The more events we attended, the more people we met. It got so familiar that we knew people at every celebration. Getting in was not even a problem any longer. We just showed up in our best outfits like we were invited. Weekends became one long party.

Graduation

The weeks leading up to my graduation in 1958 were filled with excitement. It was hard to believe that my years at Lincoln were about to come to an end. While I looked forward to moving on to college, leaving my beloved high school was a terrible loss. In all my years in the projects, Abraham Lincoln High School was the bright spot in my universe.

No matter how bad things got at home or how desperately broke we were, the beautiful campus offered a safe haven. I was more at home there than I was in my own bed. For five years, it had been my savior, my security blanket, and I was not ready to leave it. And yet, as the days passed I saw it all coming to a close.

In the final week before the great event, my mom became violently ill. I reacted by closing the door to my room and working on the speech I was scheduled to give at the commencement ceremony. I began to realize how much I depended on the public role that had become the centerpiece of my life. It gave me all the acceptance I never got at home. It was the part of my existence that I lived for. There was no way to fully express my gratitude to that school, the teachers who expanded my universe, or to the kids who I now loved so desperately.

The day before graduation, Mom took me aside and said, "Honey, I have something important to tell you." I was shocked. Never before had she approached me in this manner. I sensed something big was up. "I hardly know where to begin," she started. "Things have been so crazy ever since we moved into this horrible place. I can't imagine what it's been like for you. It's been pure hell for me. All these years of insanity are just too much to sum up in a few words. But there has been a change...one you should know about."

Tears began to fill her eyes. I reached out and took her hand. "What is it, Mom?" I asked quietly. She shook her head and said, "I've been such an idiot. I don't know how it happened. We got so caught up in the drugs we lost sight of our children." She began to cry openly. I tried to console her.

After a few minutes she continued, "I can't believe how

badly we messed up your lives. Our own lives were a living hell, but that's no reason why we should have dragged you down. It wasn't your fault. You deserved better."

I inquired, "Why are you bringing all this up now?" She dried her eyes with a piece of tissue and said, "I've quit using. I'm never going to shoot up again. I put down at the beginning of the week, and I've been sick ever since." She started to cry again then added, "No matter how bad it gets I promise you I will never let you down. I'm done. FOREVER."

I sat in stunned silence. I had nothing to say. It was such a monumental news flash, it caught me off guard. I had not even fantasized that such a day might arrive. Living in the middle of a "shooting gallery" was just situation normal. I couldn't conceive of any other kind of home life. "Does Dad know?" I asked, at last. "Not yet," she responded. "I'll tell him next time he calls from the road. It doesn't matter what he says. It's over for me. He'll have to deal with his own devils. I'll never touch that shit again."

She began to cry again. I put my arm around her and said, "It's OK. We'll get through this together. I'm going to work full time this summer and save enough money to move us out of here. We can start a new life." Then I, myself, began to cry. Years of suppressed tears poured down my face in torrents. With our arms entwined, we both wept for a long, long time. There were tears of sadness for all the lost years. Tears for the time spent in isolation, separated from one another. Tears for the unspeakable pain. It all came out.

A Great Day

The school auditorium was filled to overflowing. Proud parents, along with younger children and other family members chatted excitedly as they waited for the ceremony to begin. Everyone was dressed in their Sunday best. For many, it was the first time anyone in their family had graduated from high school. It was truly a momentous occasion.

Backstage, there was a last-minute dash to prepare for our final production. My teacher, Ray Lopez, was a blur of activity. He had last minute instructions for everyone, especially me. He said plaintively, "Please, Kenny, NO JOKES today! We have a long program to complete. There is simply no time to waste fooling around. We have speeches to give, awards to be announced, and a huge line of graduates who are going to receive their diplomas. We're on a tight schedule." He eyed me anxiously. "Do I have your promise?"

At that moment, I realized just how much I was going to miss this remarkable man. I gave him a big hug and said, "Today, no messing around. You can depend on me." He said, "Well that would be a first," then spun around to deal with the last remaining details.

I peeked out from behind the curtain to check the audience. Mom was seated in the front row with my brother and sister. She was animated, talking to everyone around her. She looked like a different person. Quitting the drugs "cold turkey" had been a huge challenge for her. Now she was beginning to experience a rebirth. I was very proud of her.

I had other things on my mind as well. I had a welcoming speech to give and another longer speech which I had written for the occasion. I didn't want to blow it.

Then the house lights dimmed at last, and I stepped onto the stage to great applause. I did not begin speaking immediately, giving myself a brief moment to gather myself.

Every school assembly began with the traditional Lincoln invocation. I had recited it so many times in the past, it was second nature to me by now. The timeless words came out of my mouth for what was to be the last time. "We hold these truths to be self-evident. That all men are created equal."

I recited the rest of the words in a space I had never been in before. I was present but in a different way than I had ever experienced. It was not just the orator in me reciting my lines. This was not just a graduation. The words seemed to find me and come out of my mouth with no thought whatever. I was in some distant universe. The sound of applause brought me back to this one.

"I want to welcome you all to the Graduation Ceremony for the class of 1958, the Mighty Imperials." More applause. "I have a couple of jokes I prepared for this occasion but since I have been assured that even one joke would result in Mr. Lopez having a heart attack, I will pass on those." I stole a glance at Ray offstage. He was blushing and silently mouthing his thanks.

"And now I would like to begin our program by turning the mike over to our class sponsor and guiding light, Mr. Raymond Lopez."

Ray came on stage and thanked me effusively for not screwing up the time frame for the program. Then he began the formal proceedings. He acknowledged our class as being "special," then turned the show over to the principal who introduced the speakers.

The rest of the program turned into a vague cloud for me. I remember receiving a gold plaque and a small scholarship from the Bank of America for excellence in Liberal Arts. Everything else went off smoothly until the principal announced, "And now we have a highly unusual award to present. It has not been awarded to a Lincoln High School student in many years. It is my pleasure to introduce the presenter for the American Legion 'Boy of the Year' Award."

In a matter of moments, the legionnaire reached into an envelope and withdrew a document. "And this year's award goes to ....KENNY KAHN. Kenny, Please come forward." The crowd rose to it feet as one and burst into a deafening applause. All I could see was Mom accepting backslaps and hugs from those nearby. She was beaming.

So was I.

Epilogue

The bizarre and unlikely events I have related in this book were but the beginning of the scrambled course I would follow in this life.

Over the next ten years, my path led me to law school in Berkeley in the '60s. In the midst of social, political and sexual revolutions, my education continued in many different directions, all of which will be the subject of my next book.

It will also cover the breaking free of America, hitch-hiking across Morocco and spending a year in Spain with expatriates from all over the globe.

You can keep track at www.kennykahn.com.

Kenny Kahn

A portion of the sales of each book will be donated to the March of Dimes.

My Dad, Barry Kahn and
my Mom, Faye (Brody)
Kahn when they first
met in 1938.

Dad, Mom and me in 1944

Below, Grandma Tillie (Rose) Brody in 1942

Top: Mom and Heavyweight
Champion Max Baer in 1945

Top right: Mom's first job at Comet's
Juice Stand in downtown L.A. in 1938

Right: Dad and Mom on Ocean Park
Beach

Below: Rich relatives—Dad's sisters
Bobby (in black) and Lil (front right)
and their husbands

Cousin Donald Field (my hero)

Girl cousins Arlyne, Tina, and Bonnie

Left: The only normal time in my life selling papers on Alsace Avenue.

Below: Dad working the "Pin Store" in Klamath Falls, Oregon.

218

Ramona Gardens Projects in 1955: Top, Ricki holding Cookie next to the Community Swimming Pool. Below, the Delgado girls (left to right) Dolores, Mary, and Rosie.

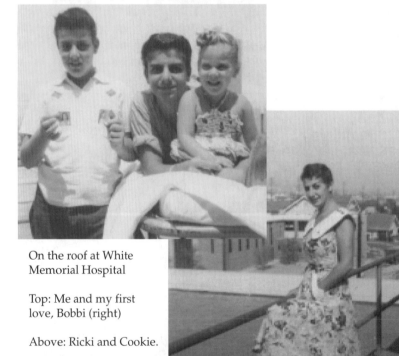

On the roof at White
Memorial Hospital

Top: Me and my first
love, Bobbi (right)

Above: Ricki and Cookie.

Right: Mom

220

KENNY KAHN
Lincoln

High School life — speech contests,
football and politics

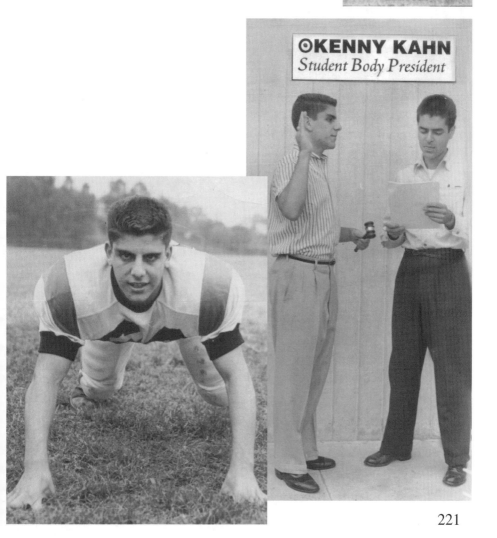

221

Lincoln High School, Ninth Grade Class of 1955

Below left, American Legion certificate
where I was named "Boy of the Year"

Below right, portrait of a graduate, summer, 1958

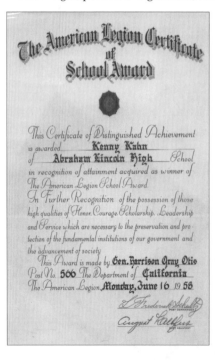

GLOSSARY

Agent
Carnival employee who operates games of chance

Alibi joint
Carnival game using a physical object, known as a "G" or "Gaff," to control the outcome of the game.

Back door
To leave an establishment without paying

Beef
Complaint by angry mark

Blow off
Mass exodus from some fair event

Booster
Sells hot merchandise

Buckets
Alibi joint with a "G" or "Gaff'; baskets

Calling
Verbal shouts to attract attention

Carny
Carnival worker

Chill out
To end a play to a mark; also Cool out

Cuttin' up touches
Sharing stories or "jackpots"

Doniker
Toilet

Enemy
Police; also fuzz; also heat; the man

Flat store
Most sophisticated carny game; also called a "Grind" store

First call on the right
The best location on the midway

Gaff
Device to control game; also "G"

Gash
Female; Broad; Chippie

George
Good. Also "Georgie Porgie"

Grab joint
Burger tent for off-duty carnies

Gypsy
To switch dice

Hanky-pank
Carnival game: lowest level of skill

Hey Rube!
Call for help during fight on midway

Hit and Miss
Piss

H.O.
Hold out: hiding money from the boss, also known as "Oats"

Jimmie Brit
Shit

Joint
Any carnival game

Jump
Show moves from one town to another

K.B.
Kick back; returning cash to mark

Knocker
Mark who advises others not to play carnival games

Lot
Place where carnival sets up

Luz 'em gayn
Let him go; a bad apple; Yiddish

Mark
Sucker: Anyone not a carny; also "mooch"

Midway
Area designated for rides and games

Mitt camp
Gypsy subculture on carnival

N.G.
No good

Oats
Funds stolen from boss

O.C.
Overcounting; Technique of false counting to make it appear mark can win at a flat store

Overcalling
One agent working to a mark some one else has called in

Ones and twos
Shoes

Patch man
Advance man for carnival; arranges for police bribes

Peek a Poke
A view of the contents of a mark's wallet

Pin store
Type of flat store utilizing numbered clothespins

Rang
Boisterous, combative mark; orangutan derivative

Razz board
Type of flat store; employs numbered board and marbles; Count store

Ruffle
Ride boy, mechanic; roustabout

Roll out
Leave a restaurant without paying

Score
Large rip-off

Shill or stick
Carny pretending to win prizes

Smash
Coins

Still date
Carnival event only: no county fair or other celebration

Slum
Cheap prizes

Spooks, Spics, Slants
Major racial groups

Store
Joint

Tender
Young

The send
Keeping a game open while the mark goes out for more money

Tip
Extremely busy action. Lots of players

T.O.
Takeover; one carny replaces another during a play to a difficult mark

Tom
Bad, also Larry; also N.G. no good

Weak sister
Epithet; attacking manliness

With it
Password for free entry to anyone working on the carnival

223

Quick Order Form

- Fax orders: 310-393-8548. Send this form
- Website orders: www.pendant-press.com
- Postal orders to: Kenneth Kahn
      330 Washington Blvd., #400, Marina Del Rey, CA 90292
- Telephone orders: (800) 431-1579

Please send_____ copy(s) of The Carny Kid
                    (quantity)

each @ $19^{95} (U.S.Dollars) for a total of $_____

in California, sales tax @ 8.25$^{%}$_____

Shipping and handling @ $5 each_____

Total $_____

Name_____

Address_____

City_____State_____Zip_____

Phone (   )_____

Fax_____   Email_____

Check no./date_____
Payment: ❑ Check ❑ Credit card:
❑ Visa ❑ MasterCard ❑ AMEX ❑ Discover

Card number:_____

Name on card:_____Exp. date:_____
For discount orders of 12 or more, telephone (800) 431-1579